THE SURVIVAL OF
"TITCH"
IN HITLER'S GREECE

ΕΥΣΤΑΘΙΑΔΗΣ GROUP A.E.
ΕΚΔΟΣΕΙΣ, ΕΙΣΑΓΩΓΕΣ & ΕΜΠΟΡΙΑ ΒΙΒΛΙΩΝ
ΚΕΝΤΡ.: ΔΡΑΚΟΝΤΟΣ 88 - ΑΘΗΝΑ ΤΚ 104 42
ΤΗΛ. 210 5195800 - FAX: 210 5195900

ISBN 960 226 583 3

Lyn Rowland

THE SURVIVAL OF
"*Titch*"
IN HITLER'S GREECE

A TRUE STORY

EFSTATHIADIS GROUP

Hitler's stormtroopers stand and watch Athens burn during the days of Nazi occupation of Greece - Athens 1941.

Contents

Introduction

SYNOPSIS
THE SURVIVAL OF "TITCH"

This synopsis reveals brief details of 'Titch' and his experiences during World War 11 in Greece.

The autobiography revolves around the life of a young Greek boy from the age of seven until he was thirteen during the years 1939 to 1944. He was nicknamed 'Titch' by the British Army 1944 in Athens.

The story of 'Titch' talks of the incredible way in which he survived his horrifying experiences during the four years of terror under the German occupation of Greece. The story revolves within the districts of Kokkinia now called Nikaia, Piraeus, Athens and England.

He talks of the way his mother and father died, and why he was separated from his sister and brother for fifty two years, and what he found when he returned to Athens from England fifty years later for the first time with the help of Sky television. He reveals the way in which he survived from starvation, having to sleep rough among the ruined buildings of Piraeus and in German cells.

The night of a raid in Piraeus by the resistance against the Germans when he was caught red handed by the S.S. and taken prisoner after they had broken his jaw with the butt of their machine gun.

The sheer horror of being dragged to an execution post and blindfolded along with three other prisoners to be executed by the S.S.

The night he was buried alive under the debris for three days in Piraeus, and the night of terror when he had to bury a dead German in a cellar.

The terrifying moment of being thrown into a large tip amongst scores of dead bodies in 1944 outside Athens and was nearly buried alive.

He tells of the summer 1944 when he was taken by the S.S. with many other prisoners from Piraeus to the Blocco of Kokkinia, now called Nikaia, to be executed along with several hundred other prisoners that were already there when he arrived.

Why he was forced to hide in the caves of the Acropolis in Athens. How he became involved with the British Army after the evacuation of the Germans at the end of 1944, and why uniforms were cut down to fit him, fought the Civil War with them in Omonia SQ and in the railway underground in Athens Dec 1944, and later they made him a sergeant.

In 1946 the army took him to England and introduced him to a new life. Details of this unique story were recorded at the time by British newspapers and American magazines. Photographs and newspaper clips are contained in the book. The book also gives a brief history of events in Greece throughout the war before the autobiography begins.

BRIEF HISTORY
OF THE GREEK TRAGEDY

WORLD WAR II 1939 - 1945

The degree of destruction and hunger Greece had suffered in World War II from three successive attacks, in the years of 1940 - 1944, by the Italians, the Germans and the bitter Greek Civil War, can only be described as that in Yugoslavia, Russia and Poland. The occupation of Albania by Mussolini in April 1939, brought a great threat to the Balkans. Greece could hardly hope to escape the general conflict that was obviously approaching, and by the end of the year 1940, Mussolini ordered his troops to cross the Albanian border to invade Greece.

In the meantime the Greek government had already strengthened the armed forces as much as possible, but the strength of the Greek army - aided by a handful of British and New Zealand troops was however insufficient to resist a second attack that was inevitable to follow by the superior forces of Hitler.

By the beginning of 1941 Greece played a gallant part against the axis. After a series of energetic counter

13

attacks, by the Greek armed forces, the Italians were forced to retreat back into Albanian territory, and this enabled Greece to win the first victory. It has been said that sixteen Greek divisions had immobilised twenty-seven Italian divisions, despite the Italian supremacy in equipment, artillery and aircraft. Five months later, the Germans came to the rescue of their Italian ally and on 6th April, 1941. Hitler launched a major air attack on Piraeus harbour across the Bulgarian border.

At this stage the port of Piraeus was very much congested with shipping. The British ship Clan Fraser was also there at the time and had on board several hundred tons of T.N.T. The Germans were well aware of the situation and their bombers were sent in. The first wave of German planes came skimming over the mast tops of the ships. Mines were dropped into the water and were followed by low dive bombers.

The explosion of Clan Fraser wrecked the port and was felt up to ten miles away, but the Piraeus ordeal was not yet over. At 2. 45 am that Sunday morning the city of Piraeus rocked to more violent explosions from other ships in the harbour. When dawn approached over Piraeus, the ships in the harbour were still burning furiously, and so was a good part of the city. Crowds of dazed, panic-stricken men, women and children were swarming up the seven mile road from Piraeus to Athens. In Athens, there were thousands of homeless refugees packed around Omonia Square. While thousands more from Piraeus and other parts sought sanctuary in the railway stations surrounded by their bundles of belongings.

Its effect on the morale of the people was shattering. Demoralised by the sudden destruction of their homes, they were convinced that the German planes would come back night after night. Most people of Piraeus and surrounding area fled to the countryside and mountains to take refuge. The port was blockaded with magnetic mines which the Germans had dropped, and as they continued their attack raid after raid, Piraeus virtually ceased to exist as a port. Its destruction caused many dead and wounded, and the loss of eleven ships along with many other small vessels. One can only describe the ordeal as horrifying, and the people of Piraeus without a doubt will bear the scars for many years to come.

By 23rd April 1941, it was a well known fact that a German invasion of the whole of the Balkans was by all odds not very far away, and the King and Greek government were forced to leave the country without any hesitation and seek refuge with the British.

The Greek Army aided by a handful of British and

Piraeus after the bombing 7th April 1941.

Piraeus, Athens 1995.
A diferent world from the world of 1944 after the NAZI occupation.

New Zealand troops could not possibly resist the Germans for long, and in a very short space of time had to evacuate and made for the Middle East. Four days later on the 27th April 1941 the Germans invaded Athens and Piraeus. By May 1941 the whole Greek territory came under Axis occupation and the country was divided into German and Italian sectors.

The atrocities and starvation committed by the Germans in the first year of their occupation were barbaric. All the country's resources were taken over by the Germans and later they introduced special occupational bank notes, and issued them freely without limits to all their military units according to their needs. This, however, led to the immediate explosion of the country's monetary system and international trade was brought to a halt which was bound to lead to food shortages and its tragic consequences. Soon after starvation began to play its' part, far more than one can imagine.

During the tragic winter of 1941/42 hundreds of thousands were dying from the slow death of hunger. The highest proportion of these victims being women children and the old who put up a tremendous struggle to survive starvation. Many were homeless and many thousands were forced to beg for food or even steal from the

Germans, or where ever they could. Many were caught and shot. Those who did survive did so purely through determination and the will to live. For many their bodies became beyond recognition. This led many people to eat any scraps of garbage they could lay their hands on. Most of it was hardly fit for animals let alone for human consumption. The discomfort from the fleas was a menace for many thousands of people.

In spite of all this, it had not broken the will and determination of the Greek people to fight back with any means possible, and by the beginning of 1942 resistance was beginning to take a massive form, which would in due course result in a direct confrontation with the enemy. It has been said that the first Resistance organisation had been founded as early as September 1941, followed at a distance by minor organisations. This stubborn resistance which lasted all through the occupation, was however a great advantage to the Allies.

The high and virtually inaccessible mountain ranges in Greece, enabled the Resistance to operate from secure bases. By the middle of 1942, various resistance groups grew in scope and intensity. Daily raids and sabotage took place, and were later followed by the regular battles in the streets with the Germans and those whom the Resistance suspected of collaboration with the enemy.

As time went on during the years of 1942-43, the Elas Communist Resistance grew in tremendous strength, and this brought a great threat and distrust to other resistance organisations as they all had plans of stepping into Government shoes if and when the Germans should evacuate from Greece. The King and Greek government in exile were completely cut off from the country, even the Greek armed forces were in the Middle East, serving under Allied Headquarters. Who else was therefore left other than the various resistance organisations to step in and fill the country's political gap? This however led to the tragedy of the bitter Civil War after the evacuation of the Germans in Greece at the end of 1944.

In the meantime, new centre of power, new leaders new mass movement and political aspiration were needed in the struggle that was about to begin if Greece was to survive. The year 1942-43 led many people to struggle for survival, as hunger and the cold winter took place like never before, combined with the atrocities committed by the Germans who later raided and burned scores of villages, innocent victims were taken as hostages and were executed as a deterrent to the resistance movement.

The executions often took place near the villages in the open fields. People were often to frightened to leave their homes in order to search for food. They were afraid of getting caught in the conflict over the increasing street battles between the Germans and the resistance. In spite of all this, various resistance organisations accused each other of collaborating with the Germans, and this also brought more bitter fighting in the streets.

In September 1943, the Italians capitulated in Athens and Piraeus and later in other parts. A large number of them surrendered their weapons and themselves to the Elas Communist Resistance. At this stage, the power of the Elas Resistance was indeed felt very quickly by the right wing resistance organisations as they all had good reasons to fear one another. In January 1944, heavy air raids were launched on Piraeus by the Allies against the Germans, causing great damage with many dead and injured. Later the streets of Piraeus were unbearable to walk on, due to the increasing stench of dead bodies lying alongside of the pavements and amongst the ruins. This however was due to the bodies being left for some time after the raids before the Germans disposed of them. Disease began to spread throughout, and the Germans feared that themselves could become the ill victims.

In April of 1944, large scale military manoeuvres was organised by Elas Organisation against the Edes Resistance. After a long series of bitter battles in the streets, the Germans launched a massive attack against the Elas troops thus, obliging them to retreat to the mountains. Some of the atrocities committed by the Germans in 1944, can only be described as barbaric and horrifying. They executed around about 80,000 people and burned many hundreds of villages, and thousands more died from the suffering of torture.

Throughout the Occupations around 600,000 people had perished, most of them from starvation and as a result of bad conditions. These figures do not include however, the hundreds of thousands who died from executions tortures, and defeat. About 400,000 houses were completely destroyed and around 1,800 villages had been totally burned down. The large harbours, railway tracks, telephone network, civil airports and bridges, had been totally destroyed.

On 12 October 1944, the Germans evacuated Athens and Piraeus, destroying anything and everything along the way. By this time the country was in ruins. In some villages and camps, dead bodies, which the Germans had left behind them, had to be thrown into large tips by the hundreds. The amount of destruction they caused during their withdrawal from Piraeus and Athens was enormous.

Three days after the German evacuation, British

troops entered the capital in the midst of demonstrations. The tragedy of the bitter Greek Civil War was about to begin. The bid to take over the country by the Elas Communist Party, and other right wing resistance organisations against the will of the people, the exiled King and government. The British Government however was in the meantime taking all possible measures to stop the country from falling into Communist hands. By the end of the month, the Elas Communist troops not only intensified their punitive measures against the collaborationist and fascist bands, but started to arrest civilian hostages, which they hurried out of Athens and into the mountains. This however, was to establish one of the main and most effective propaganda instruments in the hands of the future right wing government. Several thousands of the hostages is believed to have been executed by Elas troops, and many hundreds died as a result of bad conditions.

On 3rd December, 1944 large crowds of various resistance organisations, including many from the Elas Communist Party, assembled in Constitution Square in Athens. Whilst the demonstrations continued, a large number of the public gathered in the square to hear them. Many of which were women and barefooted children. I know as I was there at the time. Suddenly out of the blue, shooting broke out. Many dead and wounded covered the pavements. Crowds of panicking women and children scrambled the streets screaming from fear trying to save themselves.

This was the start of the bitter Greek Civil War, and continued till 1949. As from that day 3rd December 1944, until the middle of January 1945, Athens and Piraeus became a bloody battlefield between the Elas Communist forces and other organisations, the people, the future right wing governments, and the British troops.

Throughout those seven weeks, a continuation of bitter fighting took place in both cities. British troops and the Greek police fought side by side bitter battles against the Guerrillas. Most of the shops and Omonia underground railways were in ruins and were used as firing cover by all those involved in the fighting. In the meantime, failure to support the Elas Communist party and its political aims. By the people, brutal torture were being committed by Elas troops against innocent victims. It has been described by some people at the time that those tortures were worse than those committed by the Germans. In view of this, the support the Elas party and other organisations had gained by the people at the earlier stages of the war, had by now began to crumble.

Meanwhile the population had to barricade themselves in their homes, and this led them to suffer from further starvation. During those seven weeks, all life throughout Athens and Piraeus ceased to exist except for those involved in the fighting. Although the Civil War continued in the midst until 1949, by the 3rd week of January 1945, the bitter fighting in Athens and Piraeus was brought to an end.

Thousands of homeless children who suffered the pains of hunger and destruction for so long would not possibly have survived very much longer if the fighting had continued. The work and resources of the United Nations relief and rehabilitation administrations had of course done a great deal for many thousands of Greek children, but the scars of the Greek people were to deep to forget the destruction and hunger they had endured for so long.

By Feb 1945, Athens and Piraeus was beginning to come to life. Law and order was restored. Shops, cinemas, schools, public transport, and night life started to function for the first time in five years. The bright lights had began to shine throughout the capital as forces from other nations started to arrive. For many Greek people there were tears of joy in their eyes as if a new world was about to be born.

24

My story is the true story of my life during that time and begins in 1939.I make no political or moral statements just leaving the reader to reach his own conclusions of his fellowman.

Chapter 1

THE INVASION

Thisautobiography revolves around the life of a young Greek boy, nicknamed "Titch", from the age of seven to 1939 until he was thirteen in 1945. A boy who lived through horrifying experiences during the four years of terror under the German occupation of Greece in World War II, and the bitter Greek Civil War at the end of 1944. The story of "Titch" reveals many dramatic moments through the war and the incredible way in which he survived it all as a child.

My present adopted name is Lyn Rowland. I was nicknamed "Titch" by the British army during World War II in Athens, Greece. My date of birth, which I state in the book as 13th December, 1932, was also estimated and given to me by the British Army. Up to the present day I have never known my real age or date of birth.

My real name was Elias Yialouris. I was born in Kokkinia, about five miles from Piraeus in Greece, where I lived with my mother, father and sister in a small two-roomed house. My father's name was Yorgos Constantinos Yialouris, he was a seaman in a small cargo boat. My mother's name was Despina. My sister's name was Demitra and she was then about thirteen or fourteen years of age.

My father had a son by his first marriage named

Evangelos. He was about twenty five years old and lived with his aunt in a village a short distance from us. My mother had told my sister and I never to have anything to do with Evangelos but, at that time, I did not know why.

Up until the year 1939, we were a very happy family and had plenty of this worlds' goods. I was then seven years of age. In 1939 war broke out and, by the end of 1940 Greece was attacked by Italy. By the beginning of 1941, Greece played a gallant part against the axis. Single handed, she defeated the greatly superior forces of Italy which had attacked her. About four months later in April 1941, the Germans came to the rescue of their Italian ally and, launched a major air attack on Piraeus harbour - a short five miles from where we lived. My father was then at sea and we had had no communication from him for a long time. My mother was very worried as we didn't know whether or not anything had happened to him.

All through the Saturday night and the early morning hours of Sunday 6th April 1941, our village rocked to the concussion of the violent explosions from the ships in the harbour during an attack on Piraeus by German bombers. As the air-raids continued, we were forced to take a few belongings from our home and, my mother, sister and myself started to run with the crowds of refugees into the mountains. A few weeks later on 27th

April 1941, the Germans invaded Athens and Piraeus. By May 1941, the whole Greek territory was under a Double Axis occupation, and the country was divided into German, and Italian sectors. Meanwhile, our money gradually dwindled and eventually ran out.

Within weeks of the German invasion, food and other essential commodities had become very scarce. We were on the point of starvation and had no other choice but to go out begging for food. We were reduced to eating orange peelings and scavenging anything and everything that we could lay our hands on. What we managed to find was hardly fit for human consumption but, beggars cannot be choosers!

During the first year of the occupation, the atrocities committed by the Germans along with the hunger, led many people like us to struggle for survival. When the Winter of 1941 approached us, food shortages had became so bad that hundreds of thousands were dying from starvation. Our bodies were becoming beyond recognition and we, like many others, were forced to the point of death.

Late one afternoon during the Winter of 41/42, my mother and I were returning home after begging for food, when all hell broke loose in the street where we lived. The Germans and the Greek Resistance movement were shooting it out. We were then only a couple of streets away but couldn't move as flying bullets and the presence of Germans soldiers made it impossible for us to continue on our way. We ran to take cover by an old broken down truck and watched from there for fifteen minutes or more. The Germans advanced to the top of the street and we then dashed for cover and eventually reached our house. My sister was very pleased and relieved to see us. She had been on her own and was very frightened by the noise and the whining of bullets. My mother did her best to comfort us and told us to keep quiet because the Germans had returned and were now practically on our doorstep.

The firing then stopped and suddenly there was hammering and kicking at our door and through it charged some German soldiers. Meanwhile, mother had told me and my sister to hide under the bed, as she knew that the Germans were taking Greek hostages after every Greek uprising to be executed as a deterent to the Greek Resistance movement. The Germans started searching the house thinking, no doubt, that we might be sheltering resistance partisans. I was spotted under the bed and was dragged out by one of the Germans. During the ensuring struggle, my mother tried to intervene, but was hit in her shoulder with the butt of a rifle by another German.

Satisfied, that we were not hiding anybody, the soldiers went away. My mother was lying on the floor in tremendous pain, my sister and I could do nothing except cry and were still doing so as we tried to sleep that night.

Next morning, mother tried to get out of bed but found it impossible due to the pain in her shoulder and so, she was forced to stay in bed for a few days. I went out, on my own, in search of food. I walked the streets all day and even begged for food in the market, but, as most people were in the same situation, I went home empty handed. We were reduced to eating normally inedible scraps of food which were found in the gutters - anything to stave off starvation. We were entitled to a bread ration, but, by the time it was divided and given out, it was hardly enough to feed a mouse. Mother made us eat our portion but, she did without hers so that we would have something to eat later. The result was, that she became very weak through malnutrition.

We now had one bed in the house which the three of us shared endeavouring to keep each other warm. Very late one night we were awakened by a knock on the door. We thought at first that it might be the Germans again. Mother got up to see what it was, and as she opened the door, standing on the threshold was my father accompanied by two other men. You can imagine how pleased we were to see him after all this time, as at one stage we thought he might have got killed by the Germans. A little while later the two men left, and with tears of joy in her eyes mother shared the half loaf of bread with us that my father had brought with him.

That night my sister and I slept on the floor mattress in the other room so that mother and father could sleep in their bed. Two weeks later my father disappeared again. Up to this day I don't know for sure if he was connected with any of the resistance and later arrested by the Germans. His whereabouts was not known to me until some time later. At that moment in time I was too young and too hungry to understand what was happening around me as my body was becoming beyond recognition from starvation. As time passed by during those winter months of 1941/2 the scarcity of food and other supplies rapidly deteriorated and we, along with thousands of other Greek families were very near to death from hunger and the cold winter. We were forced to beg or even steal from the Germans or from where it was possible. Many were caught and shot.

My wardrobe was now reduced to a pair of shorts, one shirt and a flea ridden coat with ribbed sleeves. I had no shoes and was obliged to go about bare-footed. By the winter of 1942, it was merely a question of how much longer we could survive. It was only through strength of will and determination to live that we had managed to pull through for as long as we had. By now, it was just a matter of time as to which one of us in the family would be the first to die.

Chapter 2

THE FAMINE

One morning while mother was out collecting our bread ration, my sister tried to wake me, but was unable to do so. Thinking that I was dead, she ran down the road to get help from an old lady. Arriving at our house, she quickly realised that I was near death from starvation and tried to revive me with a cup of olive oil. Luckily this had the desired effect. She told my sister that another ten minutes and it would have been too late. When my mother returned around mid-day and heard the news, she was very distressed. I was made to stay in bed and was forced to eat not only my bread ration but some of my mothers' as well.

It started to get very cold and, as we had no fuel, my mother and sister had to chop up some of the furniture to make a fire. A few days later, I managed to get out of bed. Mother was out searching for food. My sister and I decided to chop up more furniture to light a fire. Mother returned home empty handed and collapsed on the bed from sheer exhaustion and hunger. That same afternoon, I walked the streets for several hours begging for food but to no avail, and so it was, with heavy heart, my body completely drained of energy and my feet frozen from walking bare-foot on the icy ground, that I decided to return home. It was some time before it dawned on me just how quiet and deserted the streets were.

Suddenly, shooting broke out. The Germans and Greek Resistance had encountered each other. Within minutes I was caught in the crossfire, it took no time at all for me to find my second breath and run like fury to take cover behind a nearby building. In my haste, I failed to see the four Germans soldiers guarding that particular part of the street. They grabbed me roughly by the arm and started talking to me in their own tongue but, as I couldn't understand a word they were saying, I just stared at them in stunned silence. Without warning, the Resistance opened fire on the four Germans across the street. I was made to lie on the ground whilst both parties continued to shoot it out. A short time later, this exchange ceased and all that could be heard was the firing a little distance away. I was about to get to my feet when, out of nowhere, several of the Resistance men appeared from behind the four Germans and gunned them down. Two of them fell on top of me and, as they did, their blood was splattered all over my body.

When the machine gun fire had stopped, I was still on the floor, trembling like a leaf. The Resistance men dragged the dead bodies off me. I couldn't believe that I was still alive! It was only due to the fact that I was lying on the ground at the time of the shooting that saved me from the hail of machine gun bullets. Even my rescuers were surprised to find me so after the amount of bullets they had fired at those Germans.

Events were moving swiftly as reinforcements of German troops arrived by truck at the top of the street and started to deploy themselves for a further attack. Some of the men picked up all the weapons from the dead Germans whilst another grabbed my hand and we all had to make a run for it before we were spotted by the advancing troops.

After running for a short distance, I was directed on to a safe road and then they left me. From there I made my way back home. When I arrived home, I tried to avoid my mother until I had had a chance to clean the blood stains off my trousers. I didn't want her to know what had happened as she would have worried and wouldn't have allowed me out in the future. I shut myself in the outside toilet so that I could clean the blood from my clothes as best as I could but, without success. I decided to wear my trousers inside out in order to hide the stains - they were so ragged, no one would notice the difference anyway!!

When I entered the house mother was asleep. My sister told me to leave her as she wasn't well. Sitting on the mattress. shivering with the cold, tears started to stream from my sisters' eyes as she told me how hungry she was. I did my best to comfort her and told her that I would go out again first thing in the morning in search of food. That night, my sister and I tried to go to sleep, but due to the pains of hunger and our rumbling bellies, we found it extremely difficult and lay awake most of the night anxiously awaiting daylight.

As dawn approached, I went to wake my mother to remind her that it was time to go for our meagre bread ration but was stopped by my sister. She said it was best to leave mother as she was very ill. Not realising that my sister also was in no fit state to go anywhere, I asked her to come with me to collect the bread. She tried hard to stand on her feet but, was so weak from lack of food that she fell back down again. I leaned down and tried to comfort her and told her to hold on whilst I went out to collect the bread ration. I made my way to the bakery as fast as I could. When I got there, I tried to sneak my way in to the front of the queue but was spotted by a German guard. He shouted at me as he came forward and, grabbing me by the arm, pushed me to the rear of the queue. I was lucky, if an adult had tried the same thing their bread ration would have been stopped.

I returned home with the bread some three hours later to find my sister crawling on the floor in a state of collapse and very near to death from the horror of

CHAPTER 2

hunger. After several attempts to wake up mother I
eventually succeeded, she looked at me through half
open eyes and attempted to speak but didn't have the
strength to move her lips. I quickly realised that my
mother was in a similar situation to my sister so I broke
off our bread ration and tried to force some of it into her
mouth, thinking that might revive her but it was useless,
I was fighting a loosing battle. I tried to do the same to
my sister but she was out cold. At that moment, I didn't
know whether my sister was dead or unconscious. I
became very frightened and started to panic. Tears were
streaming from my eyes as I ran to fetch the same old
lady who had revived me with a cup of olive oil.

When I reached her house, I found her door half
open and shouted to her from the steps outside but there
was no answer. I walked straight in and found her lying
on a floor mattress and took it that she was asleep. I tried
to wake her and very soon realised that she was dead. I
ran from the house and headed for the church a few
streets away, hoping that the priest might be able to help
me. When I entered the church there was no priest
inside. I came out and started running back to our house
not knowing what to do. On my way, I saw the priest and
shouting for him to stop, I ran up to him, kissed his hand
(it is customary for Greek people to do this) and

frantically told him that my mother and sister were dying. Taking my hand, he said he would go with me.

When we entered our house, my mother was crawling on the floor desperately trying to reach my sister. The priest immediately lifted her onto the bed and after examining both my mother and sister, he said a prayer. He told me to stay with them whilst he went to the church to get something. After what seemed like an eternity, he returned with a small bottle and forced some of the liquid between their lips. He lit two more candles and prayed for them.

An hour or so later, both my mother and sister began to come round, my joy was overwhelming. As the priest was leaving, he told me that they were now in God's hands and gave me a small bottle of the same liquid which had helped my mother and sister saying that I was to give both of them as well as myself a teaspoonful each morning and night. He also gave me a small loaf of bread cake, which is made of corn, and told me to wait one more hour before I fed them. I mentioned to the priest the death of the old lady and he said that he would attend to her.

By nightfall, my mother and sister were much better and were able to get up. I was so happy and relieved that they were well again that I burst into tears. I knew then that a miracle had happened and that the prayers said by the priest had been answered.

After that harrowing ordeal, we somehow managed to survive the rest of the Winter mainly by begging and from whatever scraps of garbage we could pick up off the pavements. Late one night by the end of the Winter there was a knock on our door. My mother fearfully answered the door, thinking that it might be the Germans but, to her surprise, it was the same two men who had come with my father a few months previously. Mother invited them in and, they then broke the news of my father's death. My mother was shattered by the news.

When morning came, mother and I started to make our way to the place where my father's body was being kept. Feeling as weak and hungry as we did, we didn't relish the idea of the long walk ahead of us. We walked and walked until we didn't have the strength to walk any further. Mother collapsed on the ground and we were forced to rest for some time. As we were resting, I spotted a German camp where a lorry was unloading fruit. On top of the lorry was a German guard. I told my mother I was going over to see if I could get any food from the Germans. Weakly, she tried to hold me back as she knew that people were often shot for trying to steal food in those days it was commonplace to see German lorries being attacked in the streets by the Resistance movement.

I left mother and walked towards the lorry and, as I watched them being unloaded, one of the boxes fell to the ground and oranges were scattered everywhere. I couldn't believe my luck! I rushed to pick some up when the guard fired some shots. My mother rushed over to take me away but, in doing so, was hit in the back with the butt of a rifle by one of the guards. I picked an orange off the ground and threw it at the guard. My mother was writhing in agony on the ground when a German officer appeared on the scene and realised what had happened. He then picked two oranges off the ground and handing them to us told us to leave which, we gladly did.

My mother could hardly walk because of the pain in her back but she struggled along. We shared an orange between us and kept the other for my sister. After walking for another hour or more, we finally reached our destination. It was not a pretty sight. As we were let into the building by the German guards outside, the stench from the dead bodies inside, was enough to suffocate us. Most of the bodies had been kept there for some time until the Germans could dispose of them, and were in an advanced state of decay.

We spotted my father's body but could not get to

close due to the stench. At first we had difficulty in recognising him, as his face and the top part of his body of what we had managed to see had hardly any flesh, and that applied to the rest of the bodies inside. My mother grabbed my hand as tears were running down her face and said, "Let's go home." Up to this day I do not know what sort of place that was, but I shall never forget it.

On reaching home we were very thirsty. Water was in short supply and with no money we could not afford it. We were not able to wash and drank infrequently. There were no taps in the house and the nearest pump was a few streets away. We ate our bread ration when we got home whilst the fleas continued to annoy us, running all over our bodies. Exhausted we went to sleep.

One afternoon in July 1942, my mother and I were returning home after begging in the streets when, to our amazement, we spotted a dead horse in the fields. It was covered with flies and surrounded by savage dogs which were tearing it apart. Cautiously, we approached the dead animal intent on snatching a piece of the meat to cook when we got home. The hungry dogs turned ready to attack us if we went any closer. We had no choice but to turn tail and run leaving the dogs to a kings feast and us yet another day without food.

It was only two days after the incident with the dogs

that my mother collapsed, after walking the streets once again, in search of food. We let her sleep, knowing that in her weakened condition she could do little else. That afternoon, after walking the streets for several hours and once again, with nothing to show for my efforts, I was returning home when I saw a queue of children outside a building. I joined them. I wasn't supposed to be there but I waited and, eventually was rewarded with a small piece of cheese and two biscuits.

Pleased, that for once I could return home with something, I went home as fast as my feet could carry me. My mother was still sleeping so we kept the biscuits and cheese until the following day when we were entitled to another bread ration. We could then give mother the biscuits and cheese. My sister bandaged my feet blistered from walking on the red hot pavements and then spent the next hour or so sitting on the doorstep killing the fleas on our bodies.

The next morning we tried to wake mother, realisation dawned and I passed out. My mother was dead. When I came to, a priest was standing over us. My sister's body racked with sobs. The priest lit a few candles by mother's bed and prayed. He told us that she had died from starvation and that we must be brave. He then made arrangements for the funeral.

Life must go on, and so kissing my mother for the last time, I went to fetch our bread ration. On my return, and still in a state of shock, I had started to cut the bread into three pieces when my sister reminded me that we were now only two. I couldn't think straight. For a moment I had forgotten my mother's death. After the funeral, my sister and I tried desperately to comfort each other. As we lay on the floor in the semi darkness that comes just before dusk, mother's bed stared back at us in agonising silence. The memory that not so long ago, mother had lain there, had loved and held us in her warm and tender arms, was deeply etched in our minds.

Our thoughts became so unbearable that we decided to move the bed in to the other room, trying at the same time, to eradicate the bitter hurt we felt deep inside. Afterwards, we slept on the floor mattress. With our father and mother gone, our concern and love for each other had grown far more now, as we were dependant on each other for our survival.

Chapter 3

RUNNING AWAY FROM HOME

In one particular visit to the bakery to collect our bread ration, my sister and I had set out very early in the hope that we might avoid the long queue. When we arrived at the bakery the queue was already more than half a mile long but, having no other choice we joined the waiting crowd. It must have been a good four hours later that we approached the front of the queue when, suddenly a woman in front of us collapsed on the ground and died and a scuffle broke out between the German guards and some of the other people in the queue. The guards opened fire and, in the process, two women and a child were killed. In the meantime, I had grabbed my sister and pushed her to the ground to avoid the hail of bullets. After that incident, the Germans closed the bakery.

Taking our place back in the queue, we waited, along with the crowds of women and children, in the hope that the Germans would re-open the bakery and supply us with our meagre entitlement of bread. Another two hours passed and some of the less able in the queue left in despair and returned to their homes, some of them only just managing to drag their feet as they left. The heat from the sun was terrific, and with nothing to quench our thirst made matters even worse. Tension was high and the smell of bread outside the bakery tormented us and our stomachs rumbled in noisy sympathy as we continued our long and endless wait.

Eventually, the Germans decided to open the bakery and began to serve us with our bread rations. By this time, my sister was in a bad state and hardly had the strength to put another foot forward. She was helped by two women who propped her against a wall whilst I collected our bread. Helping my sister home, we could no longer contain our hunger so, we ate the bread on the way. Knowing that she didn't have the strength to walk the streets anymore, I told her to lie down and rest whilst I went out alone.

Late that afternoon whilst I trudged the streets from one end to the other, I spotted some Italian soldiers leaning against their trucks minus their vests and shirts. They were eating fruit and, as I waited anxiously for them to finish their feast, my mouth watered in anticipation. After they had eaten, I rushed over to pick up their left overs off the ground. One of them spoke to me but I didn't understand what he was saying. Another soldier leapt down from the truck and fearing the worst, I backed away. He held his hands out, in them were an apple and a slice of melon, offering me the contents. I couldn't believe my luck, another gave me a small bunch of grapes and a couple of biscuits. I was so thrilled and excited, I started to fill my pockets with the remainder of their left overs lying on the ground. I could barely wait to get home to my sister and surprise her with my good fortune.

However, my feeling of elation was to be short lived for when I arrived home late that night, I found my half brother, Evangelos, in the house. This was the first time I had seen him for a long time. My sister informed me that he had come to stay, an idea I didn't like at all. Despondently, I took the fruit out of my pockets and divided it into three portions.

The next day Ya Ya Eleny, Evangelos Aunt who lived a mile away came to our house and said that Evangelos will now stay here as we need someone to take care of us. As the weeks went by we got to know what Evangelos was really like. He was very jealous of any affection shown towards me by my sister Demitra. He took control of everything including our bread ration and often used me to further his own ends. Often he would punish me for no reason at all when my sister wasn't home.

Evangelos had heard that the Germans were looking for young girls to work for them in the cigarette factory in Piraeus and told Demitra to apply for the job. She did and started work the next day. She was paid very little money and a hundred cigarettes a week. The cigarettes were the best part of her wages. Of course Evangelos took the money and I was made to go out and sell them on the streets or wherever possible. The price he was asking was far too high and I could only manage to sell two or three cigarettes at a time. Most people didn't have any money for food let alone cigarettes.

Often I would go home, having sold only a few, and he would punish me unmercifully for not having sold more. My sister often intervened but, she also was beaten for daring to try. Things became so bad that I was afraid to return home. On one particular occasion he had sent me to collect our bread ration and on my return, some five hours later, he accused me of eating some of it, which I hadn't. He stripped me of my ragged clothes and threw me naked into the street. I sat on the ground at the back of the house and waited for my sister's return from work. When she eventually arrived and saw me she became very angry and hammered the house door telling Evangelos to give me back my clothes or she wouldn't go to work any more, knowing that this might bring the Germans to the house which was the last thing that anybody wanted.

Another time I had been sent out with a hundred cigarettes and told that unless I sold them all I would go without my bread ration for two days. I tried to sell them but with no luck and decided to go to Piraeus. In those days there weren't many buses so you were lucky to catch one. I jumped on to one as it slowed down coming round a bend and had to hang on the door rail as I had no money to pay the fare, this being common practice then.

To my dismay, half of the cigarettes fell out of the packet and the bus was travelling too fast for me to jump off. I was terrified at the thought of what Evangelos would do to me and knew that he wouldn't believe my story. I wandered the streets, with fear of facing Evangelos when I got home overriding even the pangs of hunger.

Without warning, shooting broke out between the Germans and the Resistance. People were running about the streets desperately trying to find shelter. I ran to take cover in the doorway of a building and stood trembling with an impending sense of danger. Bullets were flying all over and bouncing on the ground only inches from where I stood. By now I was petrified and wanted to escape the situation and running started to cross the road.

I was half-way across when I was caught in the cross fire. Bullets whined all around me. One of the Resistance shouted to me to lie flat on the ground, he then rushed into the road firing his machine gun at the Germans.

However, the Germans were returning the fire and within seconds he was shot several times and fell dying a few feet from where I was lying. Just then a German tank appeared from around the corner. I kept very still pretending to be dead but as the tank neared, I was terrified and couldn't control the terrific trembling that shook my body, all I wanted to do was to get the hell out of there but, I knew I was in no position to do so as the gunner above would have opened fire at anything that moved. On the other hand I couldn't stay where I was because as soon as the tank moved it would run straight over me.

There was only one way to go, so, I slowly started to crawl, hoping against hope that I wouldn't attract the attention of the gunner above us, who still continued to fire up the street as I pulled myself under the dark belly of the tank. I continued to crawl on my stomach for several feet until I managed to reach the other side of the road and scrambled to relative safety to the back of one of the buildings where I stayed until the fighting ceased.

It was very late when I reached home that night totally exhausted from my 'adventures' and very hungry. I hesitated, not knowing whether or not to go into the house because Evangelos, by now, would be in a state of violent agitation. However, I did venture in knowing full well what was coming. It came, the inquisition, his failure to believe my story when I finally got the chance to explain. He just went berserk, eyes bulging and foaming at the mouth from sheer temper and with the speed of a madman he chased me around the room with his belt. He hit me over the head with it and when I fell onto the floor he kicked me mercilessly, I was certain every bone in my body must be broken.

My sister rushed into the house from the outside toilet and tried to stop him but he just turned and vent his fury on her. I went to bed without my bread ration as he had said I would, and tried to work out how I could leave home for good but thoughts of what would happen to my sister kept flitting through my mind.

The next morning, whilst Evangelos was in the toilet, my sister gave me a piece of bread, which she had hidden the previous night, and told me to eat it before Evangelos came in. The speed at which I was eating it should have caused me a bad bout of indigestion. I was on my last swallow when in he walked and asked me what I was eating. I naturally denied eating anything. With that, he turned on my sister accusing her of giving me something and started slapping her about the room. I panicked and ran from the house as fast as I could.

I didn't know where I was going and didn't much care,

all I wanted to do was to put as much distance as I could between myself and Evangelos. I walked and walked until I could walk no further and I stopped to rest and gather my strength. I was feeling so very lonely and depressed and very, very hungry. I tried to unravel my jumbled thoughts and, despite the love I had for my sister, I decided to run away for good. As I walked the streets that day, I ate anything I could find to stave off starvation and, as night fell, I looked for somewhere to sleep. Eventually, I found a large yard, it wasn't much of a place but, it was somewhere to lay my head and rest my weary body. The walls, I noticed, were about ten feet high and there was a gate which could be bolted from the inside. There was also a small broken down shed and so, bolting the gate, I made myself as comfortable as possible and thankfully, went to sleep. I was now about nine and a half years old.

When I awoke the next morning, it took a little while for my senses to register. Hunger was taking its toll of my body as I weakly got to my feet. I knew that I didn't have the strength or energy to walk very far but, my immediate problem was to find something, anything to eat. Thoughts of Evangelos pounded my brain and I knew I had to survive so that one day I could turn the tables on him for what he had inflicted upon my sister and myself.

My mother Despina.

My brother Evangelos.

Demitra - Titch's sister with two of her five children by Evangelos. Photo taken around 1960.

Evangelos - Titch's half brother who married his sister post-war. Evangelos was to die of a heart att. in 1962.

My ideas of revenge gave me strength and, with renewed determination, I set off in search of food to fill my stomach. I was given a handful of sultanas by an old lady but, within a short while, I began to feel drowsy and once again, the feeling of malaise set in and weakness invaded my body. I dragged my feet in the general direction of the yard, I so badly wanted to lie down. I didn't dare pass out, "Dear God", I thought, "don't let me pass out", that was the last thing I wanted, if the police found me they would take me home and, back to Evangelos. Somehow I managed to keep going and on reaching the yard, collapsed on the floor and slept the sleep of the dreamless.

Chapter 4

THE INVOLVMENT WITH THE RESISTANCE AND THE BREAKOUT OF THE GERMAN CUMP

I woke to the sound of gunfire, taking little notice as I had grown accustomed to the ever increasing street battles. However, the firing became closer and a scuffle was taking place on the other side of the wall. I could hear voices and somebody was trying the gate. I became alarmed and sought refuge behind some bins in the yard.

Suddenly, a member of the Resistance clambered over the wall and jumping down to the ground, unbolted the gate letting in another man who was carrying a briefcase. They were obviously surprised to find nobody in the yard as the gate could only have been bolted from the inside. I must have made a noise or, some sixth sense warned them that they weren't alone because, they spun round and opened fire at the shed next to the bins where I was hiding, no doubt thinking they had fallen into a trap.

Bullets whistled over my head and, panic stricken, I yelled and came out from my hiding place. The man with the gun just had time to hold his fire as he realised that it was only a small child and as they approached me, a voice shouted over the gate asking them if they were okay and to move as quietly as they could because the Germans were closing in, as indeed they were.

Within minutes, the area was surrounded. There was

a renewal of gunfire just beyond the gate and the sound of a truck screeching to a halt, no doubt carrying German reinforcements. Moments later, they were trying to break down the gate hereupon, the Resistance fired towards the gate. I scrambled back behind the bins just in time to see a German stick grenade sail over the wall into the yard.

Ducking as it exploded, shattering the bins in front of me, I wasn't hurt but, the Resistance men were not so fortunate. One of them was killed instantly with his body practically torn apart and his comrade was critically wounded in the chest and legs and bleeding heavily. Gasping for breath, he called me over and overcoming my fear, I went to his side. He told me he needed help and asked me if I would do something for him and for Greece. Confused, I agreed and upon his request, passed him the brief case from which he took some papers telling me to hide them inside my shirt. He also told me where to take them and to whom I was to give them impressing upon me that many lives were at stake if they fell into German hands.

This was to be the turning point in my future life and at that particular time, I didn't know that it would also save my life. The Germans were still trying to break down the gate, and the wounded man told me to point

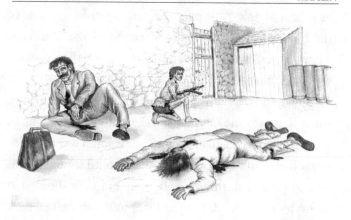

An artist's impression
        of the yard where Titch got involved with the Resistance and the Germans after he run away from home.

                                                    by Alan Morgan

his machine gun toward them and press the trigger. As I fired there was a cry from the other side and I thought that I had in all probability shot one of the Germans. He then told me to hide the briefcase in the shed and to get back behind the bins and not to come out until the Germans had gone. The Germans smashed the gate open with the aid of another grenade which finally killed the Resistance man.

Entering the yard, the Germans searched the two dead men, I held my breath and kept very quiet and hoped that they couldn't hear the thud, thud, of my heart as it beat at an erratic pace. Something dislodged one of the bins which attracted the attention of the Germans. They advanced towards the bins, their rifles cocked, shouting for me to come out with my hands up.

Slowly I rose up from my hiding place surprise spreading over the Germans' faces as I emerged. One of them started to laugh at seeing such a small boy and they pushed me out of the yard. For a moment I thought I was free to go and started to walk away but they shouted at me to halt. Terrified, I did as I was told and walked back toward them. I was hoisted into the front seat of a truck with one of their guards, then they loaded the dead German into the truck and drove off to their camp.

When we arrived at the camp, the guard sitting next to me took off his coat and started shaking it. I realised that some of my fleas had decided to try pastures new. The situation made me laugh for the first time in two years. The guard turned nasty and pushed me to the ground and a moment later, he started poking me with a stick and pointed out the way I had to go. He certainly wasn't taking any more chances!

I was conducted to a small office where I was interviewed by the Commanding Officer. He spent twenty minutes trying to interrogate me, his broken Greek unintelligible to me, and eventually he gave up. I was then escorted to a cell which I soon discovered was rat infested, The guard slammed the heavy steel door after him leaving me alone and very bewildered. There was no bed in the cell and the only light came from a

very small window. I leaned against the wall and prayed to God to let me out.

I was becoming very tired and was about to lie on the floor when three rats appeared about two feet away from me. I was terrified and started to scream. The rats scuttled back to their holes. After that, I was too afraid to lie down and so I stayed on my feet, walking up and down the cell for hours making noises to keep the rats away. When night fell, I was left in total darkness and try as hard as I might to stay on my feet, I was so tired and weak from starvation that my legs would not hold me up any longer and I collapsed onto the floor.

When I woke up the next morning, it was like a nightmare, rats, the size of cats were all around me and I had to shake two of them off my legs. I was screaming hysterically and for a moment, thought I was going mad. My loud screams brought the guard who chased some of the rats and succeeded in killing one with the but of his rifle. He picked it up by its tail and took it out of the cell. A while later he returned, bringing me a piece of black German bread. I was so hungry that I couldn't eat it fast enough. I tried to think of how I could escape mainly because I was petrified to spend another night in the cell with those rats running about. To this day, I still have a fear of anything that bears a resemblance to a rat.

I had no intention of surrendering the papers to the Germans but was very much afraid they might search me. My plan of escape was, to wait one more day in case they decided to release me or failing that, to take them to the yard under the pretence of showing them where the papers were hidden, hoping to run away when we got there.

It was about midday when my cell door opened and the guard escorted me to the Commandants office for further interrogation. As I entered the office, I saw a small table laiden with food, including a bowl of spaghetti. The Commandant knew I was starving and smiling told me that I could sit down and eat all I wanted and then be free to go providing that I told him what he wanted to know. It had been such a long time since I had seen real food that I was sorely tempted but, remembered what the Resistance man had said about a lot of people dying if the papers fell into German hands.

The Commandant then started to question me through a Greek interpreter, who was in the office with him at the time. He said that the men who were with me in the yard had in their possession a briefcase containing some important papers. He told me that they had found the briefcase but the papers were missing. He asked me if I saw what they had done with them. I denied all knowledge of their existence upon which, he said I was lying. He said that I had better tell them the truth or he would be forced to hand me over to the Gestapo. The interrogation continued, but I remained silent, and after a while, I could see that he was losing his patience with me. He then summoned the guard who took me back to the cell.

As I walked into the cell, the rats scurried to their holes! Terror became my main emotion and I started to pace the cell making noises to keep them away. When darkness came, I was so afraid and exhausted from having to stay on my feet, I prayed to God once again and, I believe he heard me for, a few hours later, the German camp was under attack by the Greek Resistance movement. As the grenades shattered the walls of my cell, I could hear machine gun fire and the German troops running all over the place. Once again, terror struck me and I began to scream but no one came to me. With all the confusion, who would hear the cries of a small boy!

The shooting continued for some time and as I stood

with my back to the wall in pitch darkness, I could hear the rats squeaking and running about the cell. Suddenly, someone came to the cell door and spoke to me in Greek telling me to stay clear of the door. They fired at the locks on the door and poured into the cell. They told me not to be afraid, because they were dressed in German uniforms, and to follow them.

We ran to the end of the corridor where we were interrupted by the German guards. The Resistance opened fire and killed them. We then climbed some steps and were helped up through a big hole in the roof by more Resistance men. After I was hoisted through the hole, more men swiftly followed as the third and last man, who was disguised as a German corporal, was being lifted through, a German guard appeared and shot him dead.

Within seconds, the Resistance men above returned fire and killed the German. They then decided to make a run for it. We run a few yards and climbed down the other side of the wall being helped by further Resistance men. They had commandeered two German lorries and an armoured car. Pandemonium reigned about us.

Several of the Resistance men were still shooting it out with the Germans as we prepared to leave and the men at the gates climbed on to the lorries. As we drove away, some of the men threw hand grenades at the Germans. A little further on, we were stopped by more of the Resistance flashing their torches at us. They were guarding the roads to stop other German patrols from entering the camp during the attack. Continuing slowly, the lorries were turned into a field as a German patrol made its way up the road. I was lifted down from the lorry and one of the men took charge of me. I was frightened even though I felt I was in safe hands.

When the Germans came into range, the Resistance opened fire ambushing the patrol. During the shooting, the man next to me was shot and, as I turned round to help him, I was hit by a bullet in my right leg. As I screamed with pain, two more of the Resistance came to my aid.

"Where are you hit, kid?" one of them asked. "It's my right leg." I replied very distressed. He then said, "Try and hold on a while". and, leaving the other man to comfort me, went off to continue fighting. It wasn't long before the firing stopped. It was all over.

As they prepared to move out, the head man of the Resistance shone a torch on my leg and said that I had been very lucky, the bullet must have spent itself on a tree before partly embedding itself in my leg. He told me that it would have to come out and, gritting my teeth, he placed a handkerchief over my leg and pulled the bullet out with his hand. He quickly bandaged my leg with a scarf and I was carried to the armoured car. Driving away, we headed into the mountains.

When we arrived in the mountains, several of the men piggy-backed me until we reached the top where we entered a large cave. Inside were more of the Resistance movement and a girl of about twenty five. I was laid on the floor and the girl, whose name, I learned, was Evthoxia, attended to my wound and later brought me something to eat. I was famished and just

tore into the food.

Evthoxia asked me when I had last eaten and I said I couldn't remember and continued to shovel the food into my mouth, and afterwards three of the Resistance and the girl sat around me and started questioning me. She asked me my name and where I lived. I hesitated to answer fearing they would send me back. She told me not to be afraid as they were my friends. Still uncertain, I told them I had no home and had been sleeping in the streets since my parents had died.

I was then asked if I remembered the two men I was with in the yard and, nodding my head, was told that they had belonged to their organisation. Evthoxia then said that they had been carrying some important papers which they had taken from a German officer and having, unfortunately been killed did I know what they did with the papers beforehand. She then went on to say, that they knew I hadn't revealed any information to the Germans.

Puzzled as to how they knew, I said, "I will tell you if you will let me stay here with you." "Of course you can", came her swift reply and, undoing the string which kept my coat fastened, I put my hand inside my shirt and brought out the papers I had been given by the two men to hide.After the papers had been examined, they jumped for joy and, as the men sent out loud cheers Evthoxia kissed me and said that from now on, I was going to be their lucky mascot.

Chapter 5

THE RESCUE OF THE HOSTAGES

The whole movement were in great spirits and celebrated with a bottle of Retsina, a Greek wine. Evthoxia told me that she had a surprise for me and sent one of the men to fetch somebody called Spiro. My puzzlement increased and must have shown in my face because she asked me if I remembered the man who acted as interpreter in the German camp. He turned out to be Spiro, another member of the organisation.

Now the pieces were fitting together, Spiro had worked for the Germans and had kept the Resistance informed as to what was going on, and that was how they knew about me. At that moment, Spiro came in and told me he was proud of me for not giving in to the Germans. I was feeling pretty pleased with myself too, and more relaxed than I had felt for some considerable time.

Early the next morning, I awoke screaming in terror after a nightmarish dream of still being locked in the cell with the rats crawling all over me whilst I was lying on the floor with my wounded leg. I came to with the soothing sound of Evthoxia's voice telling me that it was only a bad dream. She helped me to my feet and supported me as we walked outside the cave to a rock where she made me sit whilst she went to prepare something to eat.

Some of the men who were on guard duty came over to try and cheer me up. One of them gave me a bar of

German chocolate which I devoured in a matter of seconds. A short while later, the girl brought me a bowl of milk with biscuits to dunk in, a slice of bread, a piece of cheese and some black olives. It had been so long since I had had anything decent to eat, to me, this was indeed a feast. Looking me up and down, Evthoxia said, "You are so thin, we'll have to fatten you up a bit." With food like this being placed in front of me, who was I to object!

When I had finished, one of the men carried me back to the cave. He then cut off all of my hair with a pair of scissors, undressed me and gave me a good wash. I was then fixed up with clean clothes and a pair of shoes, the first decent garments in two years. I was revelling in all the attention I was being shown. Evthoxia dressed my leg with clean bandages, gave me a stick to help me walk and said I looked like a new boy. I was beginning to feel like a new boy. I spent the rest of the day admiring the view from the top of the mountain. I had a full stomach for the first time in two years and for a moment, I wondered if this was real or just a dream.

The following evening, Spiro arrived at the cave and said the Germans had been doing a house to house search for me and that they had taken hostages to be executed as a reprisal for the attack the other night.

Evthoxia told me not to worry as I was quite safe there with them. Laughingly, she said that the Germans wouldn't recognise me anyway, now that I was all dressed up. After a few weeks, my leg was much better and I was able to walk without a stick. It was now 1943.

I spent most of my time inside the cave helping Evthoxia with her work and cleaning weapons that the men had captured from the Germans, and during those months Evthoxia had been like a mother to me. A natural affection had grown between us and I became extremely fond of her, I believe she felt the same way towards me. My thoughts however, often wandered back to my sister. I had missed her very much and often wished that she was with me. I wondered whether she was still under the control of Evangelos. My thoughts were kept locked inside of me. I didn't dare say a word to anyone, in case I was taken back. I couldn't endure his cruelty again and often thought that I would rather die than live with him again.

One day, at the beginning of Summer 1943, I was sitting on the rocks when Spiro entered the cave in a great hurry. I sensed that something was wrong and after a little while, Evthoxia called me and asked me to enter the cave.

As I entered, several of the Resistance men were

sitting around a makeshift table, including Andreas, the Commander, waiting to talk to me. I was a little worried as I thought they were going to send me away. However, Andreas asked me whether I would be willing to do something very important for him. I told him that I would do anything as long as I could remain with them. He then said that what he was asking me to do was very dangerous and if they had any other choice, they wouldn't involve me.

Evthoxia stood behind me with her arms around my shoulder and asked Andreas whether it could be worked out some other way. Andreas stated that they had gone through it time and time again and that there was no other solution. Turning to me, Andreas said that if after explaining what was required of me, he would understand if I felt frightened. I told him that I wasn't afraid and, once again, repeated my wish to stay with them afterwards. Looking at Evthoxia, I could see the tears running freely down her face and knew that she was against the whole plan involving me.

Andreas explained to me that the Germans had taken twenty hostages who were to be executed on the "morrow and that two of them were from his organisation. A plan had been devised but my help was needed. Someone, namely me, was needed near the place of execution in order to blow up the machine gun which the Germans would use to shoot the hostages, whilst they attacked from the rear. It was imperative that the gun be destroyed before the attack began otherwise, the Germans would open fire on the hostages the moment they heard our fire. As the area would be heavily guarded, it would be impossible to get past the Germans before the execution took place but, a child could pass almost un-noticed. When Andreas had finished explaining, he asked me how I felt about the venture. Almost immediately my reply came and I told him that I was not afraid and that I would do what he wanted. Staring at me for a while with a look of resignation on his face, he smiled benignly and told me that I would be okay.

There was only a day in which to train me and so my instruction began immediately. Andreas brought out a hand grenade and explained how it worked and how to throw it after taking the pin out. He then took me outside the cave, measured the distance from the cave to a rock, a distance of approximately thirty five feet, and told me to practice for the next half an hour hitting the rock with a stone as many times as I could. Some time later, he emerged from the cave and watched me for a while. He told me that I had had enough practice and that I had the right idea. Taking me inside the cave, Andreas showed me how to fire the pistol which I would be carrying with me and impressed upon me not to use it except to save myself should anything go wrong. We had some target practice there inside the cave.

Next, with the aid of a drawing, he showed me how I was to get past the Germans to reach the little wall from behind which I would be throwing the hand grenades. I was to be carrying a can of water on my back and selling it by the cup - a normal practice then as drinking water was very scarce. On reaching the little wall, I was to stand behind it and wait until the Germans positioned the machine gun in front of the hostages and then, just before the German officer gave the order to fire, I was to throw the hand grenades and take cover behind the wall, waiting there until the resistance attacked from the rear. The explosion of the hand grenades would give them the signal.

Time and time again, we went through the whole plan, resting for a short while and then beginning the process again as Andreas said, just to make sure I would remember everything. Evthoxia, bringing us something to eat, turned on Andreas and, with a distraught note in her voice, said that it was real madness sending me and asked what would happen if I was caught. Andreas answered, "The kid knows how the Germans would react and can think for himself, and in any case, we have no other choice." Trying to pacify Evthoxia, I said that I would not get caught and that I would be very careful. Andreas said that if the Germans wouldn't allow me through, I was not to try and force my way in but, must return to the resistance. Once again, we rehearsed the whole operation.

That night, Evthoxia made me say my prayers before going to sleep. I tried hard to go to sleep but my brain kept ticking over and over. I kept thinking of the consequences if something went wrong and I was caught by the Germans, especially carrying the grenades. I even thought of shooting myself with the pistol because I couldn't betray the Resistance after all they had done for me. My stomach turned and sleep still eluded me. The confidence I had earlier was beginning to evaporate but, there was no way I would back out.

I was awakened very early, by Andreas, to have my breakfast and, afterwards, we rehearsed the mission yet again. He then told one of his compatriots to get the rest of the men ready to move out in fifteen minutes. Andreas put a grenade in each pocket of the jacket I was wearing under my overcoat and placed the pistol inside my shirt and, to make me look scruffy, he rubbed dirt on my legs and face, so that the Germans wouldn't suspect anything. As we were about to leave, Evthoxia put her arms around me and with a sob in her voice said, "God be with you Elias."

Outside the cave the men were standing around heavily armed. Andreas said a prayer and we moved out. One of the men helped me down to the bottom of the mountain where the German lorries were waiting for us. We were greeted by a few of the Resistance men dressed in German uniforms in case we were approached by any German patrols. After an uneventful journey, we arrived at our destination and, getting out of the lorries, proceeded a little further on foot. As we neared the place of execution, Andreas made me repeat, for the last time, what I had to do and, tying the can of water onto my back, he directed me towards the entrance and then left me.

Making my way into the open yard, I shouted, "Water, very cold water." I approached the German guard and, giving an appearance of friendliness, poured him a cup of water which he drank and actually paid for. I then began to make my way towards the main yard very slowly, and tried to sell water to the German guards inside. As I got about half way, I started to get very nervous and was terrified when one of the guards stared at me. My heart pounded with fear and, running my tongue over my lips, I walked towards him in a friendly manner and started to pour him a cup of water. He took the cup from me and as he raised it to his lips, another guard appeared and said something to him. Suddenly, he shoved the cup back at me and sprung to attention as a German officer entered the yard standing up in one of the two trucks which were carrying the hostages.

I made my way to the little wall, from behind which I was to throw the grenades, trying not to be seen by the German officer. I reached it without much trouble and stood behind it. I could only just see over the top, as the wall reached just above my shoulders. On my right, I could see the Germans preparing for the execution and to my left, the hostages were being tied up by the wall. I carefully watched the German officer who was to give the order to fire and took the grenades out of my pocket, holding one in my right hand and placing the other on the ground. I waited for a couple of minutes before the officer approached the firing squad. I then pulled the pins and threw the first grenade directly at the firing squad and, the second followed in quick succession. I dived for cover behind the wall, making myself as small as possible until I heard them go off. Things began to happen very quickly then. By now, the Resistance had

started to move in and I could hear extensive small arms fire and the crump, crump of exploding grenades.

My curiosity got the better of my fear and I chanced a peep over the wall. My heart missed a beat as I saw a soldier running straight at me. Pausing in mid run, he threw a stick grenade at the tied up hostages and, at the same time, I pulled out my pistol and fired at him. He crumpled to the ground and lay still. I only just had time to duck down as the stick grenade exploded killing many of the hostages but, we saved the remainder from the execution squad.

Andreas came running towards me shouting my name., He put his arms around me telling me how well I

An artist's impression
the day of the twenty two hostages that were about to be executed, just before Titch threw the hand grenades at the machinegun from the little wall on the left.

by Alan Morgan

had done to throw the grenades on target. He lifted the can of water off my back and told two of his men to take me back to the trucks. We had to run through the trees and had to wait for several minutes for the rest of the men to arrive at the spot where the lorries were parked waiting for us. At that time, I didn't have a clue where we were as I was too young to understand the names of places and, as I had never had the chance to go to school due to the war, I could neither read or write which added to my difficulties. A little while later, the rest of the Resistance men arrived. It was hard to believe that so much could possibly happen in so short a time.

Mounting the trucks, we left the area and headed up

the road as fast as we could. We knew that before very long, the Germans would be swarming all over the place. We drove out into the fields avoiding the roads, along which reinforcements would surely come. Coming to a halt, a scout back-tracked towards the road to see if all was clear. He soon returned and quickly spread the news that the Germans were coming, so we all took cover until the convoy went roaring past on its way to the area we had just left. When we were given the all clear, we remounted our trucks and, after a fantastic journey, eventually managed to reach the mountains - and safety.

Evthoxia ran to me with tears streaming down her face. I could see the joy in her smile as she told me how good it was to see me. We couldn't contain ourselves and we both ended up crying and hugging each other. Our nerve ends were too ragged after all that had happened for us to speak normally.

Later, as we all relaxed inside the cave, Andreas came over with the two men we had set out to rescue, and told me that they were all very proud of me and that they would like to give me a little present. They passed me a small box and, in my excitement, I fumbled with clumsy fingers in my haste to see what the box contained. I couldn't open it quickly enough. I had never received a present in the whole of my life as far as I could remember. At last, I managed to open the box and inside was a lovely harmonica. I was over the moon and for many weeks to come, my present was to give me a tremendous amount of pleasure - I still play the harmonica to this day.

Chapter 6

**EVDOXIA'S DEATH &
THE ESCAPE OF TITCH**

E vthoxia had done so much for me with such care and attention and as time passed I grew to love her as my own mother. I was so very happy and spent much of my time taking short walks on the mountains and watching the coming and goings of the resistance men from different missions. One day as I played my harmonica, Evthoxia came and sat next to me and started to ask questions about where I came from and how my parents had died. I stopped playing and standing up, I told her that I didn't want to talk about it and asked her not to press me into answering her questions. She was obviously curious to know about my life before meeting with the Resistance but she quickly realised that any efforts on her part to get me to discuss it would be futile and so, she said no more.

Early one morning we were woken by the fury of exploding shells. The Germans had launched a major offensive against us. Heavy shells were landing all over the mountain and the staccato of small arms fire was punctuated by exploding grenades. The Germans were fast advancing up the mountains and seemed to know exactly which way to come. Only one word passed from mouth to mouth as the Resistance men took cover and returned fire, - betrayal.

I made my way into the cave where Evthoxia was

issuing ammunition to three men. I had only been inside the cave a few seconds when the mountain seemed to move beneath my feet this being accompanied by deafening sounds. We knew that a shell had landed in the mouth of the cave and, as the dust began to settle, quickly realised that we were entombed. We tried to fight our panic and scramble over to what had been the entrance and tore at the loose rocks and debris with our bare hands conscious all the time that at any moment, the cave might collapse and swallow us for ever. We fought our way through the rubble and knew we were succeeding as we could hear Andreas and some of the men digging their way in from the other side.

It was then that another shell exploded nearby, and Andreas and some of the men were scythed down by shrapnel killing them. It was only afterwards that I thought about the loss of such a brave man. Eventually we managed to make a hole just large enough to squeeze through and emerged into the bright light of day covered in earth and dust with our fingers bloody from clawing at the rocks. One of the men tried to get some of the ammunition and guns out of the cave before it collapsed.

Suddenly the shelling stopped and looking down the mountain, we could see that the line of grey clad soldiers was now over half way up. The return fire from the

An artist's impression
    the day the Germans attacked the resistance on the mountain and Evthoxia
was killed with Titch at her side.

by Alan Morgan

Resistance was now only sporadic as ammunition and casualties had taken a heavy toll.

Evthoxia grabbed my hand and we ran to take cover between two large rocks. We watched in silence as the men of the Resistance continued to try and hold our position but, in our hearts, we knew it wasn't to be. Some of the men were killed when a grenade was thrown by the advancing Germans. Evthoxia told me to stop where I was whilst she went to help the wounded.

Watching the continuing struggle, I was becoming very frightened as the likelihood of capture by the

Germans increased. I felt in my pocket for the reassurance of my pistol, and looking up, saw Evthoxia fall to the ground as a grenade exploded a few feet from her. I ran to her side, and as I leaned down, she put her arm around my neck. Blood was spitting from her mouth as she mumbled at me to save myself whilst I could. Tears were pouring down my face as I screamed at her not to die but, she didn't answer. Sobbing I gently shook her, desperately trying for a response to my unintelligible mutterings. Indifferent to what was happening around me, I stayed with her staring at the blood shining bright against the waxen pallor of her face. It was a few minutes before I could pull myself together and it finally registered in my confused brain that Evthoxia was dead.

How long I sat there I'm not sure, but I was quickly brought to my senses when one of the Resistance men pulled me up and pushing me up hill told me to make my way down the other side of the mountain as the Germans were almost upon us. He said that they couldn't hold out much longer. Before he had finished talking, he fell dead at my feet from a bullet in the head. It was at this point that I lost control and I didn't care whether I lived or died. All I wanted was revenge for the loss of Evthoxia and the suffering and pain I had endured from the Germans. The Germans were nearing the top now and only a handful of the Resistance were left fighting. I was still crying but, with rage or self pity I didn't know. I was now crawling between rocks and stumbled over a dead Resistance man.

Automatically, I snatched his machine pistol and emptied the magazine at the Germans. I then salvaged four grenades from some more dead and threw them as Andreas had taught me one, after the other. I was impervious to the bullets whining around me...God must have been watching over me that day.

I had nothing left to use against the Germans apart from my pistol. Sense prevailed, I had to keep that for emergencies. I crawled into cover and made my way through the rocks over the last fifty feet to the top of the mountain. When I reached the crest, I scrambled in a mad rush down the other side into some rocks. As I paused for breath, I realized that the shooting had stopped apart from an occasional burst of firing. I burrowed into a cleft where I stayed in case the Germans above might see or hear me. They rarely took prisoners. After an hour or so, when I thought it might be clear, I started to make my way slowly down the mountain stopping to rest frequently.

It was very steep and dangerous, it must have been some two thousand feet high. As I progressed slowly downwards, a deep depression began to creep into my mind. My brain was full of Evthoxia's death but, at that moment, my worst fear was that I might get stuck half way down the mountain.

My normal instincts were somewhat impaired due to the recent upheaval I had gone through and this was quickly brought home to me when, the loose rock I was standing on suddenly gave way beneath me. For a moment, I fell in space but managed to keep my weight on my left foot catching hold of a rock above me. Balancing on my left foot, I grabbed hold of the rock with both hands and pulled myself onto a safe ledge where I rested for quite a time. It seemed an age before my shaking body came to its senses. Once again, I tried to descend but my legs were not long enough to reach the ledge below me. I looked all around and spotted a small tree in the distance and decided to try and reach that as it was surrounded by flat ground. I had, however, to circumnavigate a large rock in front of me. I started to walk sideways, like a crab, inching along on a small ledge, trying to ignore the certain death that awaited, thousands of feet below me, if I should slip or relax my concentration even for a moment. Hand holds were almost impossible and I was all too well aware of how small and fragile I was in comparison to the enormity of the mountain.

It was with relief that I reached the other side and the comparative safety of the tree. Progress became a little easier from here and I made a lot of ground before dark started to descend. As the light waned, it was almost impossible to climb and certainly far too dangerous, so I decided to spend the night where I was.

I was totally exhausted and lying down behind a rock, uickly fell asleep. I woke in the middle of the night in a .tate of panic, screaming with fear and with sweat just pouring off my body. I was dreaming that the Germans had captured me and, whilst trying to escape from them, slipped and fell down the mountainside. During the fall, I could hear Evthoxia's voice calling to me to wake up and telling me that I was safe. It was such a relief to realise that it had only been a dream. My senses were reeling and in my state of disorientation, I kept talking to Evthoxia. As my muddled thoughts cleared, I realised that I was alone and that Evthoxia was dead. Her voice in my dream had been so vivid that I couldn't get her out of my mind for quite some time, I was so convinced that she was there with me. I couldn't go back to sleep, try as I might, and remained awake until daylight.

Two days later, after a long and exhausting struggle, I managed to reach the bottom of the mountain. I was so weary and very hungry and I had no idea where I was.

Again, I went to sleep and again, I had another dream. I was so pleased when morning came so that I could get as far away from the mountain as I could. I walked for several hours in a state of deep depression. I spotted a small village in the distance and as I got closer, I saw there was a bus about to leave. I ran for a little way and only just managed to catch it by hanging on to the steps at the back. I stayed on the steps to avoid paying the fare as I had no money to do so.

Once again, my life was in turmoil and the security and peace of mind I had found with the Resistance was shattered. I didn't know where I was or where I was going and I didn't really care. All I knew was, that I just wanted to get as far away from the mountains as was possible.

Chapter 7

THE MEETING WITH NICHOLAS
AND HIS DEATH

A fter travelling for many miles, we arrived in the suburbs of Piraeus and after jumping off the bus, I walked the streets in search of food. By night fall I managed to reach the sea port of Piraeus and decided to remain here as there was more likelihood of finding food in a large town. What I didn't know, but was very soon to learn was that Piraeus was more heavily occupied by German forces than any of the other places I had so far experienced. Although I hadn't eaten for four days I was still in pretty good condition after my time spent with the Resistance, my immediate problem was that of finding somewhere to sleep.

After walking several streets, I spotted some ruined buildings that had been bombed in a previous attack on Piraeus harbour by German bombers in April 1941, and finding a quiet spot inside, made myself as comfortable as possible and slept through the rest of the night.

On waking, my first thoughts were of my empty stomach. I was ravenous and knowing that finding food in any shape or form was an impossibility, I decided to try and sell my small pistol on the black market. The marketeers sold bread by the slice at such an exorbitant price that gold was cheaper to buy. I walked the streets until I found a place where food and other essential commodities were being sold on the black market. I approached two men who were selling bread and after a long discussion and much bartering, I exchanged my pistol for two slices of bread. I knew the pistol was worth much more but, being so hungry, I had no choice but to accept their offer.

As the day became darker, I began to make my way back to the ruined buildings where I had spent the previous night but, walked into a skirmish between the Resistance and the Germans. People were running in the streets to take shelter. I took refuge in one of the ruined buildings behind some debris and waited for the fighting to cease.

Carefully, I moved my body but my feet shifted some loose rocks which created a noise. This attracted the attention of the Germans outside who obviously thought that some of the Resistance were taking cover inside and they opened fire with their machine guns. I hit the floor staying as flat as possible and all the time I shivered like a leaf with fear as the bullets bounced inches from where I was lying.

Luckily for me, it was dark. After firing a few bullets they shone their torches amongst the debris and left. Not long after, I could hear Greek voices coming from outside and the Resistance running about in the street. I stayed where I was and waited for the fighting to cease hoping to escape the general conflict. An hour or so later I finally decided it was safe enough to sleep.

As time passed by during the summer months of 1943, I continued to sleep amongst the ruins of Piraeus and ate anything I could find in the gutters and the few scraps of food that were given to me when I had to beg. By the end of the year the fighting became more intense. I had to take cover when walking the streets in case I got caught in crossfire between the Germans and the Resistance. The lurking menace of death was for ever present.

The clothes on my body were, by now, very scraggy and torn and, once again, I was covered in fleas. My shoes had long since worn out and been disposed of. I became very thin and illness from malnutrition and living rough soon resulted. I couldn't go home and having no one else to turn to I made out as best I could. I didn't know for how much longer I could go on and it was only a matter of time before I would die from starvation.

The strength to walk the streets in search of food deteriorated rapidly and I was forced to stay within the confines of the ruins for several days. As I slowly gave up the will to live, I often wished that I was dead and prayed to God to let me die or else to give me the strength to go on. It was now September 1943 and I was about ten years old.

On the third morning of my illness, I awoke after a very confused dream and my clothes sodden with sweat. There were many voices in my dream all trying to speak to me at the same time and Evthoxia appeared in flashes and was calling me by name. The dream had seemed so real that I was to think about it for many days to come. Within a few hours I began to feel a little better and managed to get to my feet. Still weak, I walked slowly to the entrance of the ruins and stood there for a short time and allowed the feeling of pleasure at being on my feet once again wash over me. Looking around, I saw a priest walking towards me from across the street and making my way over to him, I kissed his hand and asked him if he could spare me a little food. He said he didn't have anything on him and as he started to walk away, he turned around and said, "Come with me to the church, and I will see what I can do." I followed him like a shadow to the church a few streets away.

He spoke to me gently asking my name and where I lived. I hesitated before answering but eventually told him that my home was in Kokkinia and that I had had to come to Piraeus in search of food. With that, he gave me a large slice of bread and a drink of water and told me that I wasn't in any fit state to be out in the streets and that I must go straight home after I had eaten.

Afterwards, I kissed his hand, thanked him for his kindness and leaving the church I made my way to the outskirts of Piraeus in further search of food.

It was at this stage of the war that the Italians capitulated and surrendered to the Elas Communist Resistance and, as I walked the streets that day in search of food, I saw Italian soldiers marching unarmed in massive numbers with their hands held above their heads and I assumed that the war was over. I approached an old man in the street and asked him if the war had ended. He looked at me in a strange manner and said, "It is just the beginning."

As I continued my search for food, I met another boy of about the same age as myself in the market place near the port of Piraeus and after a long conversation I found out that he too had been orphaned and was sleeping rough amongst the ruined buildings. We agreed to stay with each other and pool our resources as regards to whatever food etc, we could beg, steal or borrow to alleviate our struggle for survival.

We arranged a meeting place in one of the ruined buildings of Piraeus where we could meet at night if ever we were split up for any reason. His company had comforted me very much at the time and I was delighted that I had found a friend in a similar situation to me.

Returning to the ruins that night, we sat and exchanged stories before going to sleep. He told me how his mother and father had been shot by the Germans outside his home during a Resistance raid against the enemy and how, during the raid two armed men rushed into his house to take cover from the Germans. At the time, he had been in the shed next to the house and had been watching through a crack in the wall. It was when his mother and father appeared outside calling him that the Germans came from the side of the house and opened fire on them and they dropped dead on the doorstep in front of his eyes.

When I asked him how he had managed to get away, he said that he had been so frightened of what he had seen that, whilst the men inside the house were shooting it out with the Germans, he sneaked out of the shed by the little trap door and had just kept running. I asked him when this had happened and he told me that it had taken place several days previous.

Without warning he burst into tears and started to talk to his mother as if she was there. I consoled him as best as I could and tried to get him to go to sleep but he would not and kept on talking to his mother. I felt so helpless and sorry for him that I started to cry as well.

When I woke the next morning, he was still asleep. I

hesitated for a moment or two, unsure whether or not to wake him for fear that he might not be in his right mind but, after a while I decided to risk it. As I was about to wake him he started to cry in his sleep and shaking him gently, I told him to wake up. When he opened his eyes, it took him a little while to realise where he was and who I was, however, a little later, he seemed quite normal. Trying to make conversation, I said to him that we must go out and search for food and he nodded in agreement.

We spent the best part of the morning in the suburbs of Piraeus and later we walked further out towards Kokkinia. I realised that I wasn't very far from home and naturally started thinking about my sister and how I was longing to see her again, but, I knew that this was not possible because Evangelos would kill me if ever he laid eyes on me again. I said to my friend, whose name I learned was Nicholas, "Let's go back to Piraeus as we won't find any food here." As we turned to make our journey back, we heard shots coming from some distance away. I told Nicholas that we had best get out of here in case we were caught in the fighting. Walking along the road, we spotted German trucks coming towards us travelling at a very high speed. There was no doubt that they were making their way to the area where the shooting was coming from.

I immediately ran across the road and took cover by the side of a building. I called out to Nicholas and told him to hurry. At first I thought that he hadn't heard me and called to him a second time, I called again and again and told him to get off the road but soon I realised that he was completely ignoring me. He stood at the side of the road and waited for the German trucks to reach him. For a moment I thought that he had lost his mind and I began to wonder what he was up to, and then, as the German trucks got closer to him, he stuck his hand out and gave the Germans a 'V' sign. The trucks didn't even bother to stop, they just drove straight over him! The trucks kept on going as if nothing had happened. I made my way to where his body was splattered at the side of the road. It was in such a mess that I started retching and had to walk away from it.

By now, I could hear a lot of machine gun fire only a short distance away and I made my way back to Piraeus as fast as I could. Although I had only known Nicholas for a short time, I felt that his death was a great loss to me and, arriving back in Piraeus, I went straight to the building that Nicholas and I had shared for the last two nights. As hard as I tried, I couldn't go to sleep, I just kept thinking and thinking of the way the Germans so callously run over him with their trucks as if he had been no more than an animal. The tears started streaming from my eyes but eventually, I cried myself to sleep.

Chapter 8

THE FIRING SQUAD

few weeks later in October of 1943, I was again very ill from hunger and was forced to stay yet again inside the ruins for a few days. Then late in the afternoon of the second or third day, just as it was beginning to get dark, I managed to get on my feet as shooting started outside and German troops were running past. I took cover behind some debris near the entrance just as the resistance opened fire, with machine guns from the street opposite, shooting two Germans who fell dead within fifteen feet of me. I was now very low and felt that I could not go on living in these conditions any longer. I had had enough and made an attempt to come out of the ruins during the shooting in the hope that I would get killed. I had lost all hope of surviving.

It was now dark and on my way out of the ruins, I tripped and fell over two dead Germans that were killed earlier. At the same time, I heard German voices in the distance. I became very frightened and crawling back amongst the debris, stayed there until the firing ceased. During the disturbance, my thoughts were to strip the dead Germans of all their valuables and to sell them on the Black Market for food.

At long last, I emerged from the ruins and managed to get the dead Germans boots off which I hid inside the ruins. Creeping back to where they lay, I took some money out of their pockets - a mere sixty five Drachma - and hid it in my shirt. I undid their holsters and took the pistols hoping to sell them along with the boots. I was about to go back inside the ruins to hide the rest of my bounty when the flash of two German torches shone on me from about twenty five feet holding the two pistols and, as the Germans got closer, I could see by the silver runes on their collars that they were members of the S.S.

They started talking to me in German but I couldn't understand what they were saying. One of them grabbed the pistols from my hands and then pushed me roughly to the ground. I slowly got to my feet and then spat on his coat, whereupon he hit me in the face with the butt of his machine gun. I fell to the floor, my mouth pouring blood and I felt that my jaw was broken - Even now, my jaw seems dislocated and occasionally it clicks when I am eating - They then made me walk with them, pausing only to pick up the two rifles that belonged to the dead Germans. They were holding both my arms and I was escorted to their headquarters that were stationed nearby. They thought that I knew who was responsible for the death of the two Germans.

On reaching their headquarters, I was thrown into one of the cells. I found difficulty in trying to sleep but, I must have nodded off because some time later I awoke

An artist's impression
of the night he was caught red handed by the S.S., whilst he was taking the pistols of the two dead Germans.

by Alan Morgan

screaming hysterically. I seemed to have gone out of my mind. My cries of distress brought in the guard who tried to calm me down.

119

A few minutes later, I was myself again. As the guard was about to leave the cell, I asked him for something to eat and in broken Greek, he told me he would see what he could do. Minutes later he returned with a slice of bread. I crammed the bread into my mouth but the pain from my broken jaw forced me to eat slowly. After a while, I lay down on the floor and went back to sleep.

The following morning, I was taken to the Commanding officer who spoke in Greek. I was questioned about the death of the two Germans and asked who my accomplices were and where they could be found. I answered that there had been nobody with me and that the Germans soldiers were already dead when I found them. He then asked me what I had done with their boots to which I denied all knowledge. He said, I suppose you didn't take their pistols either. He went on to say that unless I revealed the names and whereabouts of the people responsible for the death of the two Germans, I would be shot the following morning. He asked me where I lived but I remained silent. My silence obviously annoyed him for he called to the guard and took me back to my cell.

As I was being taken from his office, he repeated his warning to me to tell him otherwise I would be shot. When I was taken back to my cell, I kept thinking of the firing squad I would have to face the next day. I knew what it was going to be like because I had seen others executed before. I had now reached the stage where I did not fear death - I would rather die than face further starvation.

It must have been mid-day when the guard brought me a bowl of soup and a piece of bread, and he told me that this was my last meal unless I decided to tell them everything about the death of the two Germans. If I changed my mind, I was to bang on the cell door. That night, I tried hard to sleep so that I wouldn't think of tomorrow.

Prior to the execution I was interrogated once again by the commanding officer. I stood frozen to the spot and couldn't speak a word. He lost patience and told the guard to take me outside. When we got outside, there were three other men tied up by the wall blindfolded. I was dragged next to them and they tied my hands to a wooden post by the wall. They then tied a handkerchief over my eyes and walked away. I could hear sounds of rifles being cocked, as I held my breath, I prayed very briefly that I should feel no pain. As they fired, I was not hit by any of the bullets and, for a few seconds, I couldn't believe I was still alive. The handkerchief was taken off my eyes and my hands untied. The guard was walking me

121

An artist's impression
  of the day Titch was taken to be executed along with three others, but have survived the ordeal.

by Alan Morgan

away from the wall, and as he did so, I could see that the other men had been shot. I was escorted back to my cell and no explanation was given.

I was fed once a day which was more than I managed walking the streets. Interrogation took place twice more and by now, they were convinced that I was concealing the identity of those responsible for killing the two Germans.

Late in the afternoon of the fourth day, I was taken out of my cell by two guards to an armoured car and placed on the back seat between two S.S. men armed with machine guns. I didn't know where we were going or why I was moved. I thought that perhaps I was being taken to another camp for further interrogation or to a prison camp to be interned there. We must have been driving for half an hour on a long stretch of road with trees lining either side of it, when suddenly, we were attacked by the Resistance and a hand grenade was thrown in front of the car. The armoured car turned over sideways. I was shaking from the blast of the grenade but, somehow, wasn't hurt. The driver was killed instantly.

Whilst the S.S. men who had been sitting next to me returned fire, I sneaked away from behind them and run towards the trees. I ran for quite a distance into the trees but, my legs were shaking and gave way beneath me. I was completely shattered and was, by now, so low that I could run no more. I heard an explosion and took it that the car had blown up.

Eventually, everything was quiet and I found myself a spot under the trees and fell asleep. When I awoke I couldn't remember where I was or how I came to be there. I sat on the ground for a while with my back against the tree. My mind was very confused. Later, everything became a little clearer.

I made my way through the trees and on reaching the

main road, walked for several hours hoping that I would soon reach a village or town. During my walk, I had to dodge German trucks several times but, I finally reached the outskirts of Piraeus. I had to avoid the main streets and kept to the side roads in case the Germans were looking for me.

With what was left of the money I had taken from the dead German, I decided to have my hair cut in the hope that the Germans would not recognise me. I looked around for a barber shop outside which I stood trying to make up my mind whether to use the money for a haircut or to buy some food. After a few minutes thought, I decided to keep the money and to buy food with it.

Walking to the top of the street, I saw people running to take shelter and knew that another battle was about to take place between the Germans and the Resistance. I wanted to run but there was no where to run to. Unexpectedly, I was approached by two armed Resistance men who told me to get off the streets.

I knew then that I could not afford to get involved in anything for fear that the Germans would recognise me if I was caught again.

Chapter 9

**THE DEAD GERMAN IN THE CELLAR
AND THE BOMBED CHURCH**

By now the inevitable shooting had begun. I ran round the corner into the next street only to face head on, German reinforcements deploying into the street by the truckful. I only just had time to dart into the doorway of a cafe out of view. Bullets bounced off walls and pavements in all directions. I was shaking like a leaf as they ricocheted off the walls only inches from my face, one missing me by a hair's breadth but scraping through the lapel of my coat. Pushing back, as far as I could, into the very small doorway, I was suddenly hauled bodily inside the cafe by a young boy of about sixteen. "What are you doing out there," he said, "trying to get yourself killed". and, as if to echo his words, a hail of machine gun bullets splintered the door. "Lucky for you that I pulled you in when I did or you would be dead by now." Thanking him for what he had done, I quickly explained how I had nowhere to go and how I had been living to which, he said, "Well, you can stop here with me if you like."

I asked him what his parents would say to my staying here and he told me that they had been killed by the Germans. Feeling more secure, I asked him if he had any food to spare upon which, he produced a small loaf of bread and shared it with me. We moved across to the window and tried to see what was now happening outside. The fighting had died down a little and only sporadic firing could be heard on the street.

Without warning, there was a knock at the back door. My heart missed a beat for at that time, everybody answered the door with trepidation, but the boy, calmly told me to stay where I was and went to see who was there.

To my surprise, he opened the door to admit three heavily armed Resistance men and greeted them as though they were life long friends. They moved over to the centre of the room and quickly shifted a table and threadbare carpet to reveal a trapdoor into the cellar. The three men disappeared into the black hole and the boy dropped the trap above them. He called me over to help replace the carpet and table and told me that one of the men was his brother and that they were hiding until the Germans left the area.

It was then that we heard troops moving about outside so we went back to the window to see what was going on to make so much noise. We could see the Germans searching the house opposite and one soldier turning round, spotted us watching them. He crossed over and started to bang on the door. My nerves quickly departed and I begged the boy to hide me in the cellar before the Germans found me, trying to explain that I was wanted by them. The boy just laughed and said, "What would they want with a kid my age?" I tried to explain that I had just escaped from them two days ago, but all he said was, "Don't worry if they ask questions, just say you are my brother."

The knocking on the door had increased to hammering now as the suspicion of the soldier must have been growing the longer we took to let him in.

I am sure he was trying to break the door down with the butt of his machine gun. The boy opened the door and the soldier marched in, his eyes searching everywhere, suspicion written all over his face. He started to look around and as he crossed over to the table, I noticed the boy quietly shut the door so as not to attract the attention of the other patrols outside. The German pointed his machine pistol at me and told me to move the table out of the way. I did so and then he indicated the mat and as I bent down to move it, the German let out a gasp and fell to the floor. The boy had come up behind him and knifed him. Quickly the boy pulled him over and stabbed him again in the stomach to make sure he was dead.

I don't know who was most surprised, me or the German, I didn't get time to ponder on it. "Quickly open the trap", said the boy, and as I did so, he shouted down to the three men below to stand clear and, with a heave, sent the dead German tumbling into the hole. He then told me to go and lock the cafe door to stop anyone from walking in and surprising us. A few minutes later, the Resistance men emerged from the cellar and talked to the boy and turning to me, told me to keep a look out for any trouble.

I had only been watching a short while when they called me over and the boy explained that he must leave the cafe for a while to help the men escape the area. In the meantime, I was to go into the cellar and bury the dead German as best I could just in case a search was made for him. He said that I would find a shovel down there and two lit candles which would last me until he returned to help me.

As I started to descend into the cellar, the men began cleaning up the blood stains on the floor. As I reached the bottom step, they threw the blood stained rags down to me and told me to bury them along with the German. With that, they closed me in. My first thoughts were to strip the body of any valuables before I buried him but I soon realised that the others had beaten me to it and so I began looking for the spade. I knew that the candles wouldn't last very long either so, I started to dig right away. I hadn't been at it very long, when I heard heavy machine gun fire coming from outside the cafe. I dropped my spade and listened when suddenly, heavy boots ran overhead. My head spun, my brain was in a turmoil, to say I was frightened was an understatement. To be caught in the cellar with a partly buried German was not my idea of fun. I sat on the floor and kept very still, my ears strained for the least little sound, I hoped that nobody could hear the pounding of my heart, even my breathing seemed to echo from wall to wall.

Everything had now gone quiet but I waited for about another fifteen minutes and hurriedly started to dig again. My main worry now was the candles burning out and leaving me in the dark with nothing but a dead German for company.

I finished my task in record time and found myself covered in sweat and dirt, gravedigging is not a task for small boys! By now, I was down to the stump of one candle and by the increasing darkness, I knew that it would soon be gone. I went up the ladder and tried to open the trap door but it would not move. I gave up and rested. Just as the last candle flickered briefly and died, I decided to have another go at the trap door. By now, the boy had been gone for at least two hours and I was beginning to worry that he would not come back. I flung myself at the door eventually lifting it with my hand. After a considerable

131

struggle, I succeeded in opening the trap door halfway and, as I pushed harder, there was an almighty crash as the table on top of the trap door keeled over. Thankfully I emerged into the darkness of the cafe. Anything was preferable to that black hole I had escaped from. I tried to get my bearings and edged slowly away from the table and stood in something wet. My stomach churned as I felt it and realised that it was blood.

I couldn't decide what to do, whether to stay where I was or to get out of there as fast as I could. I edged further across the room and fell over a body. I recoiled in horror and then fell over another one. As my sight adjusted to the gloom of the room, I realised what the running and gunfire had been above me in the cellar. The boy and the Resistance men had all been killed. All I wanted to do now was to get away from the place anyway I could. I made for the front door but when I got to it, somebody was talking outside. I for one wasn't stopping to find out who.

I made my way back across the room, carefully stepping over the bodies, making my exit through the back door. Once outside the cafe, I walked several yards through the lane finally reaching the main road. I walked for a few miles until I could find some suitable spot amongst the ruins to lay my weary head.

Next morning, I was again on the streets with the daily routine of trying to find something to eat. I was lucky that I found several dry orange peelings in the gutter. I wasn't always that fortunate. As the day wore on, I used what little money I had to buy a small piece of bread. I was conscious all the time to avoid the main streets as much as possible just in case some observant German should recognise me, as it was not so long ago that I had been their guest. I decided to do the one thing I had so far avoided doing.

I had to go into the centre of Piraeus where I stood a better chance of finding food, even the fleas on my body looked starved. How I hated them! I will never forget the long and lonely nights I spent amongst the ruined buildings of Piraeus.

How I had managed to survive those winter months from malnutrition and in such a bad conditions only God knows. It was now January 1944, and I was now about eleven years old but, I felt I had lived twice that amount of time.

I know that I couldn't expose myself too much on the streets of Piraeus in case the Germans might be looking for me but hunger is a hard taskmaster and keeps you hard at work. So, taking the risk, I went to the market place where a few people paddled their wares on the black market.

On my feet I now wore part of a German coat I had

ripped with a piece of broken glass. I had tied it like a bandage around them in a vain attempt to keep my feet warm.

On reaching the market place, I went from stall to stall begging for scraps and left overs but I was either ignored or cursed as food was short and people were in no position to help me. I decided that I had no alternative but to steal something if I was to survive and walked round and round waiting for an opportune moment. I found a stall where a man was selling bread. I waited patiently until another man came to buy some bread and whilst he bargained with the vendor I snatched a slice from the counter and ran like fury, dodging the crowds of people who were out and about, and so made a safe getaway.

I was still walking the streets when night fell and a sudden air raid came. People scattered everywhere before the British Allied Forces started dropping their bombs. I took refuge in a doorway as the first bombs started to explode nearby. I was scared to death but decided to take a chance of getting to a church, a priest asked who I was but at that moment, a nearby exploding bomb rocked the church. I dived headlong under a wooden pew just as the church received a direct hit. As the roof and wall caved in I was knocked unconscious and all was peacefully silent.

During my unconsciousness I was certain that I was

An artist's impression
 of the cafe where Titch had to bury a dead German in the cellar.

by Alan Morgan

dreaming. It is very difficult to put into words. I dreamt
that I heard the voice of Evthoxia calling me with a voice
as if in an echo chamber and, as I started to come to, I
could hear her voice urging me to push the stones away.
And in my semi-conscious state, I did as she bid me. I felt
as if I was waking from a nightmare and after resting for
a little while I eventually struggled to my feet.

Ruin was all around me. A lot of the church had been
destroyed and it took me a time to realise what had

*The church in Piraeus near the port where Titch was buried alive after two
bombs have hit it by the allies Jan. 1944. Now it has been rebuilt.*

happened and where I was. The blow to my head had
given me amnesia for a while. The only thing that seemed
to be clear in my mind was Evthoxia's voice. I began to
regain my memory and my brain started to function
again. I didn't know for how long I had been trapped
under the debris. I moved out of the church and down the
road was a man standing outside of a bombed out shop. I
asked him how long ago the church was bombed and
could hardly believe my ears when he replied, "Three
days ago." As I turned to walk away, the man's voice was
one of concern as he saw the poor state I was in. He told
me to go home and let someone see to the wound on my
head.

Walking away I felt around the wound on my head. My hair and face were caked in dried blood and my clothes covered in dust. I had to do something about this or it would attract attention on the streets. I entered a ruined building to try and clean myself up. I ripped a piece of my shirt and kept spitting on it to make a moist rag to wipe the worse of the blood off myself. Then as I stood up to dust myself off, I found what was casing the putrid smell around me. It was sickening, there were dead bodies some of which were split in half. I quickly got out of there and headed down the road. I hadn't gone very far when I stumbled over a solitary boot. Picking it up, I just as quickly dropped it when I saw what was left of a leg inside. The smell from it made me urge.

I continued walking through the streets with depression and hunger for companions. It had been four days since I had last eaten and then only a slice of bread. My health was far from good.

The day drew on and I was stumbling along forgetting everything except hunger. Even the Germans were temporarily forgotten. The next day, I felt somewhat better and after tremendous effort, I managed to get up on my feet although I was still too weak to go in search of food.

As darkness fell, I decided that I had to get out of the place. I couldn't stand the squeaking of the rats running back and forth through the debris and the foul smell from the decaying bodies I'm sure increased my illness.

I had come close to vomiting several times. I was staggering down the road until I cold go no further. I just had to rest and did so inside another of the ruined buildings. The smell in here was as bad as the smell in the ruins I left earlier and so, after an hour or so I tried to sleep but the sudden running of boots going by made me wary. Something was going on with so many Germans running about and within minutes shooting broke out. Not long after, a grenade exploded near to the entrance of the ruins.

I was shaken but not hurt but the wall against which I had been leaning started to crumble from the blast. I moved along from it to the wall opposite all of the time finding my way by feeling the rocks as it was too dark to see.

As I crossed the floor, I felt a dead body and recoiled in shock for a moment but just as quickly got over it. Death and destruction were all around me and one became hardened to it in time. As I reached the walls, the other one collapsed and I was glad that I had moved away from it in time.

The shooting ceased and I tried to settle down and sleep but my mind would not let me. Evthoxia was haunting me. I had grown to love her like a mother and she had shown tremendous affection for me. Fifty three years later the memory of her loss is still with me as if it were only yesterday. As dawn came, I thought of searching the dead body for anything of value to sell on the black market for food. As I got close to the body, I could only see the bottom half of him and a hand sticking out of the debris. His head and chest were covered by paving slabs but his boots were in excellent condition and taking them, I hoped I could trade them for food.

I checked his wrist for a watch but that was smashed and so left it. I let his hand drop and only then noticed a ring on his finger. I tried all ways to get it off but the body had swollen and made the ring very tight. I picked up a stone and smashed it down onto his finger in order to release the ring. Encouraged by this I took some of the debris off his body and searched his pockets for anything else of value. All I found was some keys, a handkerchief, a few coins and a box of matches. I tried to get at his tunic pockets but the stones were too heavy and I had to leave the rest of the corpse unsearched. Taking off my coat, I gave it a good shake removing some of the dust and hopefully a few fleas as well, and wrapped the boots in it. Eventually, I made my way to the black market and traded both boots and ring for bread which I desperately needed.

Somehow I managed to survive the last couple of months of the winter 1944, but my ordeal was not yet over. One day whilst walking the streets of Piraeus still searching for food during the summer of 1944, I happened to remember the boots I had hidden in one of the ruined buildings the night the SS broke my jaw. I decided to take a look and with rising hopes, I immediately made my way there. The boots meant money on the black market and money meant food. I was working it all out as I made my way to the ruins.

When I reached the area I searched around and found them where I left them. I wrapped the boots in my ragged coat to stop prying eyes seeing what I had, as it would have meant certain death for me if I was caught again by the Germans.

I made it out of the ruins and kept to the side streets to avoid any German patrols. What I didn't know was that the Germans and the Resistance were about to have another showdown. As I turned the corner to another street, I sensed something was wrong. There wasn't a soul in sight and as realisation dawned on me, I heard gunfire in the distance. I crossed the road, and as I turned the bend by one of the ruined buildings that was bombed by the Allies in January 1944, I walked straight into a German patrol. I panicked and dropped the boots and coat at their feet.

I thought my time was finally up and I shook as fear took a hold of my body. The nearest one to me grabbed my arm and yelled at me in German, another grabbed the boots off the ground and started questioning me but didn't understand what they said to me but the tone they used said it all. Just then we heard heavy machine gun fire close by and the German let my arm go as some of them scrambled for cover.

I decided to make a run for it because I knew that if I was taken in, I would be recognised and it would be the end of me. I had only managed to run about twenty feet when they fired a burst ahead of me and shouted to halt. I froze on the spot. I knew from past experience that the next burst would definitely hit me and so I turned to face them raising my hands in the air.

Chapter 10

THE INTERROGATION BY
THE THREE GERMAN OFFICERS

As I made my way back to the German patrol, the shooting intensified. Just as they had menacingly bunched around me, the Resistance opened up with machine guns and two of the patrol died instantly. As the remaining two returned the fire, I fell to the ground and tried to shield myself at the side of the dead Germans. It was only the fact that they had gathered around me that I was saved from the onslaught of the machine gun bullets.

The noise all around me was terrifying. I thought I would go mad, even worse, was the thought of going back to those rat infested cells. I think I began to cry and moved my head closer to the dead German's chest to avoid the bullets bouncing only a few feet away. As I moved, I saw a grenade on him and, carefully grasping hold of it, crawled on my stomach towards the ruins intent on using it as a means of escape from the two Germans still shooting it out with the Resistance. I needed a good aim at their position for I knew I couldn't afford to miss. I pulled the pin and threw ducking my head until the blast wave washed over me. It landed on target killing the other two Germans.

Whilst I watched, the Resistance men dashed from doorway to doorway towards the place the grenade had exploded. I prayed they wouldn't shoot me by mistake in the confusion. I stayed flat on the ground until they were close enough for me to shout at them not to shoot as I too was a Greek. Sadly, none of us knew that the Germans had already surrounded the area and as they approached me the reinforcements opened fire from all directions. The two men didn't have a chance and died where they stood. Once again, I resumed my passionate embrace of the pavement between the German corpses.

The firing ceased and German troops ran over to examine the bodies, they soon found us and hauling me up, marched me off to a truck around the corner. As they pushed me over the tailboard I could see other prisoners aboard. Within the next twenty minutes more prisoners were put on the truck.

The German guards mounted and covered us with their machine pistols. With a lurch we drove off escorted by armoured cars. On reaching the German barracks, we all dismounted I was separated from the other prisoners and later, taken to a small cell on my own where I was left for ten days and nights, my only contact being the guard who once a day, brought me a cup of water and a slice of black bread.

On the third day, I was taken to the commandant's office for interrogation. He could speak Greek and accused me of helping the Resistance. He continuously

An artist's impression
    of the final interogation... taking with many others to the Bloco of Kokkinia
August 1944 to be executed.

by Alan Morgan

demanded to know with which organisation I operated
and their whereabouts. I just kept repeating that I didn't
belong to the Resistance and only happened to be at the
place of shooting quite by chance.

He then handed me my coat and telling me to put it on
said, "It is your coat, is it not?" to which I replied, "Yes".
He then pulled out a pair of German boots from behind
the desk and asked where I got them from. I told him that
they weren't mine and I didn't know anything about them.

147

With this, he banged his hand on his desk and shouting told me to stop lying. He said one of the ambushed patrol had survived long enough to tell what had happened and that I was suspected of having thrown the grenade.

"Well," he snapped, "What have you got to say?" I stood trembling all over, feeling sick inside and trying not to cry for fear of what would happen if they knew for sure it was me. He yelled again, "Well, yes or no!" I answered "No, it was the Resistance."

However, this did not satisfy him, he kept up the interrogation for I don't know how long. Eventually he broke me down and I was crying from fear, self pity and sheer exhaustion. I only just remember being dragged back to my cell. I fell in a heap on the bare floor - beds were not a luxury allowed, so I pulled my coat tight around me and fell asleep where I lay.

The next day, I was again summoned for interrogation, the same questions repeated over and over again. What organisation did I belong to, where was the hideout. Tell him what he wanted to know and he would forget the incidents of the grenade and boots and even spare my life. Again I told him that I was nothing to do with the Resistance and that it was only fate that I was there at the time of the ambush. After further questions it was evident he didn't believe my story but at that moment I didn't care. My head was filled with the rushing, roaring noise that drowned out all other light, and sound and I crumpled to the floor. When I opened my eyes, a heavy ache filled me, my limbs were numb but there was pain in my arm. A German doctor stood at my side. I think I had been injected. I was pulled to my feet and taken back to my cell.

It was about 2 weeks later when they escorted me and some other prisoners out along the corridor into an enclosed courtyard. We were made to stand in line by some trucks guarded by heavily armed soldiers. There must have been forty men with me all supposedly connected with the Resistance before their capture. We were kept waiting some fifteen or twenty minutes and during that time were not allowed to move or talk. One man was belted with a rifle butt for daring to whisper to a comrade. Before any other incidents could occur, the commandant appeared and orders were given to mount the trucks. As we moved into line to climb onto the tailboard, I thought then that this was my last hour and that we were being taken away to be executed.

I didn't feel in the least afraid to die, in fact, I felt that they would be doing me a favour. I don't know how long we drove for, I know that it seemed a long time until we entered another camp. It took a little while to realise that we had been transferred. As we dismounted two S.S. officers in immaculate black uniform came towards us dogged from behind by a plain clothes Gestapo man steering a ragged prisoner who I think was a Greek. As he got closer, the Greek pointed out two of the men standing in the line next to me. They were immediately pulled out of line and pushed into the S.S men's car and driven away. We never saw them again. I was taken in turn to the man from the Gestapo and was photographed although at the time I didn't know why and I was much puzzled by the idea. I was then put back in line and eventually the whole group of prisoners were photographed. It must have been too much for one of the prisoners. He must have lost his mind and just went berserk attacking one of the guards. He was shot dead within seconds by the guards.

The remainder of us were put into small groups and taken to the cells, but as they reached me, I was taken to a cell on my own if one could call it cell. It was little more than a box room without windows, just bare walls and a steel door. I was to spend several days here in complete darkness until I was brought out for interrogation.

When I entered the Commandants office, I was approached by an S.S. officer. The other German officers had their backs to me. As they turned to face me,

I felt a cold chill run through me as recognition of the two men washed over me. It was the same officers who had twice before interrogated me, once, when the Resistance broke me out of the camp and, the other occasion, when I was caught with the pistols I had taken off the dead soldiers in the ruins.

As they moved towards me, one said, "Well, we meet again!" By now they were fully convinced that I was well connected with the Resistance movement. I had no doubt that, from now on, nothing was going to be pleasant for me.

The interrogation continued with the same questions again and again. I was numb from the cold and privations I had been through and no matter how much I denied belonging to the Resistance, I was not believed. Later, I was taken back to my cell but, when the door was opened, panic rose inside me like a serpent coiling round me, making it hard to breathe. The dark cell was overwhelming. I lost control and screamed from naked fear but the guard struggled and managed to force me inside leaving me with my nightmares in the dark.

It was some time later when I was trying to sleep that I heard piercing screams from a cell further down the corridor. I guessed that some of the prisoners were being tortured. The screams continued and I became more and more frightened in case they would eventually start on me.

Again, I was interrogated but this time, by the two S.S. officers. My interrogation was translated by the commandant who spoke very good Greek. They fired question after question at me and I just repeated my earlier statements of having no knowledge of what they were on about.

One of them grabbed me and twisted my ear and said, "We have enough evidence of your activities in the past twelve months to shoot you where you stand. However, because of your age, if you co-operate and tell us what we want to know, you will be spared. If not, you will be shot!"

They continued to shoot a barrage of questions at me, first through one man and then through the other. Again they wanted to know about the ambushed armoured car when I escaped from the S.S. Again I told them that we were ambushed by the Resistance and I had managed to run away. "You are lying!" he yelled, and struck me across the face which sent me sprawling across the floor. Trying to get up my head started to spin, and, mercifully, I passed out.

When I came to, I found myself on the floor of my cell with a guard by my side trying to revive me with a cup of water. I had woken from darkness into darkness. I was to spend a further two weeks in the cell with the only daylight I saw for half an hour a day when I was escorted into the open air. I was interrogated twice more during this time with many promises of good food, better accommodation and no more being left in the dark if I would tell them what I knew about the Resistance movement. The alternative being the firing squad.

By this time, I didn't give a dam about anything. I had prayed every day to God, my only solace between the hunger and isolation. My strength was gone and I could endure no more. "Go to hell," I yelled at them. I had given them my answer. The next few days passed by like some unreal picture. Things happened but failed to register in my mind, until on the morning of the third day, I was hauled out of the cell and taken outside with some other prisoners to stand against some trucks. As I stood in line, I surveyed my immediate surroundings and could see that most of the other prisoners were in a really bad state and had difficulty in standing on their feet. No doubt that this was caused through the tortures they had endured during interrogation. We were made to board the empty trucks by the S.S. and I think everyone sensed that this was our final journey. Our thoughts were confirmed when we reached our destination which was a large field.

As we got out of the trucks, my eyes briefly glanced around for a few seconds and immediately realised we were in Kokkinia and only a mile or two from home. As we were escorted inside the grounds we were split into different groups and some of us were made to sit on the ground by the collaborators who were there to assist with the executions.

The Germans had several machine guns posted around

An artist's impression of the Bloco at Kokkinia Athens. The scene of horror 17th August 1944. Some of the men were pointed out by the masked informer and were shot on the spot by the Greek Collaborators. Other were escorted in groups by the Germans to the wall on the right and were machine gunned down.
Several hundred were executedthat day.

by Alan Morgan

the perimeter. There must have been several hundred prisoners there. It was a hot day, and with nothing to quench our thirst made matters even worse. Tension was high as the executions went on and on and on. The smell of the burnt cordite was blown on the wind with the cries of the dying. The men were being lined up in groups and mown down. The ground was soon red from the victims blood.

155

Chapter 11

THE EXECUTIONS OF KOKKINIA

I heard someone calling my name through the jumble of noise around me. I turned cautiously wondering how on earth in a place like this, anyone could know me. It was a pleasant surprise, as among the doomed men, I recognised a man from the mountain cave stronghold where I spent some of my time with the Resistance.

He was trying hard to talk to me without attracting the attention of the guards - but, the hubbub of noise from so many men and the distance that separated us, made it difficult to understand. He overcame this problem by sending messages in relays down the line of men until it reached me. It soon emerged that he and some of the other men were working out a plan of escape for me.

My hopes soared but I soon came back to reality when a German officer approached my line and casually picked out ten or fifteen men at random for execution. Again my luck held as the officer and guards moved away with their unfortunate victims. One can only describe the ordeal as being similar to a game of Russian roulette.

Some of the men explained the plan they had in mind for my escape. A disturbance at the far end of the ground would be started to distract the attention of the guards at this end whilst the men near me would shield me as I went over. It was worth a try, I was told, because the Germans were going to shoot us anyway and therefore, I had nothing to lose. Within minutes later the disturbance started, and, as planned the guards moved down a few feet with their backs to us. The men around me moved into action and within seconds I was helped to get on the other side of the perimeter.

I crawled onwards for several feet until I reached a small bush. There still seemed a long distance to cover before I reached the next clump and, every inch of the way, my brain was waiting for the searing pain that told me a bullet had hit me. Sweat was pouring from me and all the time my ears strained to hear the shout of alarm. I ran like I had never ran before with the energy of naked fear giving me strength. It seemed like ages before I managed to reach a safe place where I considered myself safe enough from view. As I tried to regain my strength, my thoughts brought me to home.

The more I realised I was only several miles away, I just couldn't make up my mind as to what to do. Eventually after a great deal of thought I decided not to go home.

I feared having to face Evangelos again and what he might do to me due to my disappearance for so long. I dismissed the idea out of my mind almost immediately, in spite of my longing to see my sister Demitra. A little later I reached the main road to Piraeus and decided to go there in search of food.

On my way I had to take cover several times amongst the trees at the side of the road to avoid the German patrols. As I continued my journey, my legs began to tremble from lack of food and proper rest. It wasn't long before a black mood of depression had overtaken me. I thought the chances of surviving much longer was very remote indeed.

When darkness came and all was quiet, I started my journey to Piraeus more from the urgent request my body gave me as to its need for food to keep me alive. As I continued I heard shouting and a small explosion somewhere in the distance. I took cover once again, and was fully aware of the dangers if I should ever get involved in any further conflicts. I waited for an hour or so before I made my way once again. I walked about a mile, and came upon what was left of a wrecked German truck. I assumed that it was a result of the shooting and explosion I had heard earlier.

I decided to investigate with the hope of finding something that I could sell on the black market for food. I was finding my way more by feel than sight. I felt a hand hanging out of the door. I was shaken at first, but soon realised it was the hand of a dead German. After a considerable struggle I managed to force his body out of the truck, and as I did, the full force of his weight fell on top of me knocking me flat to the ground. As I fought my way from under his body I began to notice more stiff shapes lying all around me and soon realised that they were more dead Germans.

Panic welled up inside me, my brain screamed to get out of here before reinforcements came and caught me. The other part of me told me to strip the dead and take anything of value to trade on the black market for food. I started to search the body of the dead German near me and found three hundred drachmas in one of his pockets. There wasn't much else of value except their clothes.

I took off his boots and as I tried to remove his jacket, one of his arms was just attached to his shoulder by a thin strip of flesh and took it that the blast of the explosion I heard earlier must have ripped it off. I managed to remove most of his coat with little trouble, but had to rip his arm off to free the rest. I didn't have the courage to take the arm out of the sleeve so I ripped the sleeve off with its horrifying contents still inside. I checked his holster but there was no pistol there. Like always whenever was possible the Resistance took the weapons from the Germans after an attack.

I wrapped the boots inside the jacket and made it look like a bundle not to attract any suspicions of what I was carrying should I get stopped by anyone. A lot of people in those days carried their few possessions in this way. During my journey hunger forced me to knock at the doors of several houses and beg for food but, as with most people, the situation was desperate and they were as hungry as I was. I had began to give up hope, when an old lady called me back and gave me a handful of raisins.

When I arrived at Piraeus I found what I thought was a safe spot for the night amongst the rubble of a ruined building. I tried very hard to go to sleep but I just couldn't. Fear began to grow all over me with depression and hunger for companions once again. For a while I toyed with the idea of going back home but the fear of Evangelos I dismissed the thought, in spite of my longing to see my sister Demitra.

The next morning I decided to take the boots to the marketplace and trade them for food trying all the time to avoid the presence of any Germans. During my walk about I met another boy about my age and he looked more starved and covered in fleas than I was. As we walked around the market place we exchanged words and later became good friends. He told me his name was Spiro and that his village outside Athens was burned down by the Germans. I asked him about his mother and father and he said his father was shot by the Germans and his older brother was taken prisoner. He told me that he didn't know where his mother was or if she was alive or dead.

Later he told me how hungry he was. I told him that I had something I might be able to trade for food. After bargaining from several stalls I managed to trade the boots for half a loaf of bread and a handful of biscuits. I then suggested to Spiro that we go inside one of the ruined buildings to eat as I had to keep off the streets in case I was recognised by the Germans. He asked me what I had done and I told him that I had just escaped from execution in Kokkinia and it was too long a story to explain and left it at that.

His company at the time had given me some kind of new hope of survival. The next day I said to Spiro I could not stay in Piraeus long as it was too dangerous for me if I should ever get involved in any further conflicts in the streets between the Germans and the Resistance. At that moment his immediate answer to me was that we should go to Athens. I told him that I didn't know the way, and he replied that he did.

We had a little chat and discussed our plan as to what we must do in regards to our desperate needs for food and survival. We decided to sleep inside the ruins throughout the afternoon in order to strengthen our weak condition for our seven mile journey to Athens by night. This of course would decrease the risk of German activities on the roads. We had to walk very slowly due to our weak condition from lack of food.

It was dark when we arrived in Athens and made for Omonia Square where we slept for a couple of hours inside one of the stalls above the underground railway. We woke from the sound of noise and a lot of activity around Omonia square by the S.S. and Greek collaborationist battalion guards. We became very alarmed and chanced a peep from above the counter but, we just as quickly made a dive for the floor to take cover.

We both were very frightened at the time especially me as I had a good reason to be. I was fully aware of what would happen to me should I get involved with any further conflicts as the possibility of recognition was always there. The fear of death was forever present no matter where you went. However, Spiro's company was giving me an enormous comfort and the will to survive. An hour or so later when it was all quiet we decided to get out of there and started once again our search for food. Hunger kept us hard at work if we were to survive. Most of the garbage we had managed to find was not fit for human consumption but hunger on such a scale had left us no choice. We tried not to swallow it too quickly and kept on chewing it to make it last a little longer.

A couple of days later I realised how exposed I was to the Germans or any involvement with further conflict in street battles. I said to Spiro , "Let's go back to Piraeus it's too dangerous here." "No more than Piraeus." came his reply. I told him that there were no ruined buildings in Athens like there is in Piraeus to hide or sleep in should we need to escape from any street battles. He said, "We can sleep up in the Acropolis, it is safe there."

As we climbed up there, we found some small caves and slept in one of them for the night. We continued to sleep in the Acropolis for several weeks with our usual routine in search for food whenever it was possible. Sometimes we would come down to the city by night to search for food due to a lot of disturbance and high activity of German troops during the day. Sometimes we would hear voices and men running about in the distance as we tried to sleep. Whether they were Germans or Greek Resistance we didn't bother to find out. I became very much accustomed to this sort of thing a long time ago. During the September weeks of 1944 we continued our normal routine in search for food from the little strength we had managed to force out from our weakened condition.

On the second week of October 1944 we became very ill from malnutrition. We were confined in the cave for a few days with nothing to eat or drink just the annoyance from the fleas on our bodies. At that point of time I thought our time was up. We tried to exchange words but found it very difficult to communicate. We became dazed and confused as to what was happening to us. Our minds were not functioning normally. On the fourth day of our illness I said to Spiro that we must go out and look for food or we would die. He tried hard to get to his feet but just as quickly fell back down again.

At this stage I took stock of my condition, and felt that one of us must search for food or we would both die of starvation. I told him that I must go out and search for food for both of us, and he must stay there until I returned in a few hours time. "OK" he replied, in a dazed manner.

My main concern at that moment was Spiro's health and whether he would still be alive when I returned. .His company and friendship had given me some new kind of strength and determination for his survival as well as mine. I started staggering down from the Acropolis and made for the general direction of Constitution Square with the hope of finding some food.

When I eventually managed to get to the black

market place I felt so weak I found it difficult to put one foot in front of the other and I began to lose my balance. My head started to spin and I collapsed at the side of the pavement. A man who was selling food on the black market from a stall across the street, came over to me and appeared to show some concern about my health. "What is wrong with you, little one?" he said. "I am hungry." I mumbled. He told me not to move and left me. Moments later he returned with a slice of bread, some raisins and a cup of water. He told me to eat the bread and after I rested a little, to go home as I was in no fit state to be on the streets. When he left me I consumed half of what he gave me and put the other half in my pocket for Spiro.

Half an hour or so later I regained a little strength from my rest and went to his stall and thanked him for his kindness. I asked him if I could keep the remaining water in the cup to give to my friend when I got home as he was close to death from hunger. Drink that yourself," he said, "and I will fill it up again for your friend. I was so overwhelmed I just couldn't believe my luck. I made my way home to the Acropolis picking a few scraps of garbage off the ground along the way so as I would have a little of something to chew later.

Suddenly there was pandemonium on the roads from a large convoy of German troops evacuating from Athens. I scrambled for cover at the side of a doorway to a building and watched them as they went roaring past. A little while later there was hardly any German activity around. I asked an old man up the road, where all the Germans had gone and he said they had gone back to Germany where they belonged. Meanwhile I continued to make my way to the Acropolis with the hope that Spiro would still be alive.

When I eventually made it back to the cave I took it that Spiro was asleep, but I soon realised when I tried to wake him that he was more dead than alive. It took me about ten minutes to get him to open his eyes. When he did, he didn't seem to recognise me at first or know where he was. Starvation along with the bad conditions which we were forced to live for so long, our lives by now were hanging by a thread.

An hour or so later I finally managed to bring him around by having to force a little water and bread in his mouth, slowly but surely he was becoming more aware of my presence and who I was.

After the war the thought often came home to me as to whether he would have died in that cave if for some reason I failed to make it back there that day. Two days later we both felt a little better. I told Spiro that I thought the Germans had left Athens and we would now be able to look for food without fear on the streets. I asked him if he felt well enough to walk. "Yes." he replied. "Come on, then." I said, "Let's go down there and see what is happening. When we got to Omonia Square there were no more Germans to be seen anywhere, but there were a lot of Greek people around. The sense of freedom was felt by everyone like a new breath of fresh air. This however was to be short lived.

A few days later British troops and later others entered Athens in the midst of demonstrations. Now that the Germans had left, hunger for power from the left and right Resistance groups was demonstrated in the streets of Athens.

As the weeks went by, the left group started to arrest thousands of collaborationists who were hurried out of Athens and into the mountains where most of them were executed. This, however, brought fear to the Athens population in spite of the presence and security from thousands of British troops stationed in the capital. For many thousands of civilians and the old who were still dying from hunger and the suffering of the horrors from the occupation just did not have the stomach for another war. At this point of time the writing was on the wall that a Civil war was by all odds not very far away.

In the meantime Spiro and I continued our search for food. Due to the German departure we decided to sleep in the city whenever possible. Within days of the British troops entering Athens, Spiro and I approached Omonia Square. Suddenly a group of Greek policemen were trying to catch some of the homeless children roaming around Omonia. Some of them were in very bad condition from malnutrition and homelessness just like we were. Due to my concentrating on what was happening around me at that moment I forgot about Spiro. As I turned to see what was behind me, I saw him being taken away by one police officer amongst other children. By this time I grasped what was happening and managed to get away from there. Once again my life was shattered by the loss of Spiro. For a little while I felt that his company had given me a new lease of life. Our friendship was strengthened tremendously in the short space of time that we knew each other, due to the bad conditions we were forced to live in. Depression, starvation, homelessness, the fear factor, the Germans, and the illness now and then from malnutrition took us very close to our death several times. All this brought home to us the need for each other for our survival and we came to care for one another like brothers. That night I felt it was not safe for me to sleep in Omonia Square and went up the Acropolis.

The next morning I woke up with panic and sweat. When I discovered that Spiro was not there I started to look for him outside the cave but soon remembered his capture by the Greek police. At that moment I felt that my mind was not functioning properly. Malnutrition started to affect my mind as well as my body. I felt my stomach and soon realised it was swollen from malnutrition. However, this was nothing new to me for I came very close to death in this way from starvation in 1942. I became very alarmed and feared dying. Now that the war was over and the Germans had departed from Greece, I felt the need to survive after all I had gone through.

Once again I started my search for food to build my strength. When I finally arrived near Omonia Square there was a lot of activity around by British troops and pandemonium by the Greek police rounding up stray homeless children. I was aware of what would happen to me if I was captured by the police, and kept my distance. That day I kept away from the centre of Athens and made my way to the outskirts through the back streets. Eventually I found myself lost. During my walk I came across a large open grave and a handful of soldiers with shovels burying a lot of the dead bodies the Germans had left behind them. Which country the soldiers' uniforms represented I don't know. I was too dazed and hungry to pay very much attention. There must have been a hundred or so corpses' and they were in a very bad state of decay. The stench was so bad that those who were burying the bodies were wearing masks.

At this point of time my health once again started to deteriorate very quickly and everything in front of me seemed to move from one side to the other, just like a ship in rough waters. I lost my balance and collapsed on the ground amongst the corpses'.

During my unconsciousness I was mistaken for dead and was recognised as another corpse amongst the pile. I was then thrown inside the large grave along with the other corpses'. A little while later I became semi conscious and started to move my body. At that moment I heard someone above in a loud voice, but I was too dazed to grasp what was happening around me.

When I gradually regained my consciousness and opened my eyes, I took stock around me and started to scream for my life like never before. As I looked above, shovels were lowered down to me by some soldiers and I was lifted out. I don't know who was more shocked at the time of what had happened me or the soldiers. I didn't hang about to find out and moments later after they had given me a little water to drink I ran away from there due to the stench.

It was some time later that this horrifying incident

registered in my mind of the possibility should I have not gained back my consciousness at the time I did, I would have been buried alive with all those corpses.

That grave has been on my mind haunting me for fifty years. More so than all my other war experiences, but then, my childhood life and death throughout the occupation has been some kind of Russian roulette.

In the meantime my first thoughts were of finding some food to stay alive. I was so hungry, I was left with no choice but to knock the door of several houses and eventually was rewarded by a lady with one huge slice of bread and butter with a sprinkle of sugar on it and a cup of milk. To me this was indeed a feast. I was then directed to the road for Omonia Square and eventually managed to get there.

By now it was getting dark and I was so tired from my last experience and the long walk. I just didn't have the strength to go up to the Acropolis and decided to sleep in one of the stalls in Omonia Square.

In view of the German departure from Greece I took it that the war was now over and there were better days to come from now on. I soon learnt that this was not so and another war was about to start from the enemy within.

The Civil war that was to come was at this stage just

An artist's impression
   of the day Titch was thrown into the tip alive, among the dead and was very near of being buried alive with hundred or so corpses.

by Alan Morgan

bubbling over waiting for someone to light the fuse. As I tried to sleep that night the memory of Spiro was going through my mind and how much I have missed his company.

Later I became very alarmed when I was woken by someone in plain clothes in the middle of the night with the nozzle of his pistol in my mouth and kept telling me not to make any noise.

In the meantime there was a lot of activity in the

175

square and armed men running about everywhere. Seconds later he removed the pistol from my mouth and replaced it with his hand and told me to keep very quiet. I became a little frightened at this stage as I didn't know who I was dealing with here. At that moment I heard gunshots coming from a little distance away. Just then the man decided to leave me.

It was pitch dark and I was unable to grasp what was happening out there, and besides I somehow felt I didn't want to know any more.

During the November weeks of 1944, I became a little more knowledgeable of the country's political problems. One day during my search for food I saw a man in one of the back streets of Athens being dragged away like an animal by a group of armed Resistance men, and two women from a little distance away shouting "Burn all those collaborators alive." Those weeks I witnessed several similar incidents of this kind. By the last week of November I had no choice but to restrict my movements due to my health and kept within the vicinity of Constitution Square, the Placka and Omonia.

Chapter 12

THE INVOLVMENT WITH THE BRITISH ARMY AND THE CIVIL WAR

Now that the Germans had departed from Athens, the black market traders had more goods at their disposal if one had the money or anything of value to trade with. As for myself I had no choice and my only means was to beg, steal or take whatever garbage I managed to find on the ground. Although it was not fit for human consumption, after hunger on such a scale for such a long time, it was live or die. A few days later 3rd December, 1944, I made my way to Constitution Square. When I got there I was confronted with demonstrations from various armed Resistance groups.

During the demonstrations a large crowd of the public gathered around to hear them. Many of them were women and bare footed children like me. Whilst the demonstrations continued several armed Greek policemen passed me and stopped a few feet from me to my right.

Moments later out of the blue the Greek police started to fire at the demonstrators. This caused a lot of panic and confusion not only to the crowd but more so to the demonstrators. Seconds later the area became a battlefield. No-one at this point knew who was shooting who.

Many dead and wounded covered the pavements as

179

we all scrambled for cover screaming from fear trying to save ourselves. I started to run with some of the crowd in the general direction of Omonia Square. I for one was in no fit state to run anywhere and soon fell to the ground. Just then one lady stopped to help me up but soon started to run for her life when two people amongst the crowd fell dead at our side from gunshots.

I was very weak but very much determined to survive after all I had gone through. I managed to struggle to my feet mainly from fear of being left behind. I struggled to keep up with a handful of the crowd ahead of me until we reached Omonia Square. A few people ahead of me took refuge in the hotel occupied by the British troops. I followed them in and as I stopped for breath my head started to spin. I so badly needed to lie down, and for a moment I thought I was going to die.

I managed to sneak inside the reception desk and curled underneath the bottom shelf. A minute or so later my head started to spin like never before and within seconds I passed out. How long I was unconscious that night, and when I was discovered from under the reception desk I will never know. When I finally opened my eyes and took stock of my surroundings with my confused mind, I started to scream from fear. By now my mental health had very much deteriorated. A British army doctor accompanied by two soldiers came to my aid and a moment or so later I was injected. This made me a little dazed which sent me back to sleep. Some time later when I finally opened my eyes, there was a British soldier standing by my makeshift bed in the corridor of the Hotel, on the first floor. He then went to fetch the doctor.

Moments later the army doctor arrived bringing with him another soldier and the Greek interpreter that was employed in the kitchen who brought me a bowl of soup and two slices of bread. They seemed to be concerned about my health. When did you eat last the doctor said, "I don't know, I don't remember." I replied.

After I had eaten, one of the soldiers took my measurements with a tape and said, "We are going to make you some uniforms." In the meantime they stripped me of my flea ragged clothes and gave me a good bath. This was the first time I had a bath since before the war. Afterwards they dressed me up with a pair of pyjamas three times larger than my size. They also gave me a bar of chocolate and asked me how I felt now that I was all cleaned up. "OK, thank you." I replied. They then carried me into one of the single bedrooms down the corridor. They said I had to stay in bed until I was strong enough to walk.

Just then I heard gun shots coming from outside. The soldier said, "Don't be afraid." and that I was safe with them. For several days my mind did not function normally, and every now and then I was confronted with fear and confusion. I started to scream in my sleep in the middle of the night. When the army doctor and some of the troops entered my room they found me sweating like a pig. A moment or so later I was given some tablets to take which sent me back to sleep. My illness continued in that way for several days, so I was told later.

A week or so later I felt well enough to get out of bed and started to walk about in my room. Just then, in walked the soldier who took care of me from the start, with my new uniform around his arm, and a new pair of socks and shoes. With his broken Greek we had just about managed to communicate a little. He told me his name was Jim, and I told him mine. He then said that the army would like to call me "Titch" if I didn't mind. "OK." came my reply. He told me to put on my new uniform. When I did and looked at myself in the mirror, Jim sensed my concern of the uniform being a little large for me and said, "You are very thin from malnutrition at the moment but it will be a perfect fit when we fatten you up a bit."

He asked me if I felt well enough to go downstairs

with him and meet the rest of the troops. "Yes." I replied. "Come on then Titch," said Jim "Let's go down and give them all a big surprise." He took me down to the mess room and introduced me to all the troops while they were all having dinner. As we walked into the mess room loud cheers came from the troops.

Jim said "Are you hungry, Titch." "Oh, yes." I replied. "Sit down then." said Jim, "while I go and get our dinner". While Jim went to the kitchen, all the troops just couldn't take their eyes of me. When Jim returned and placed the lovely meal in front of me, I started to eat as if there was no tomorrow. "Oh, steady on." said Jim. "Eat slowly or you will be ill again."

As the days passed by everyone was so friendly and very concerned about my health and eager to help me. At this point of time I somehow felt more secure and a little more relaxed than at any other time throughout the war. I had a full stomach for the first time in years except the little time I was fed by the Resistance. But even then no comparison to the kind of food that was available to me from the British army.

While the civil war continued outside the Hotel, the horrors of my past kept haunting me and every now and then it became very difficult to register in my mind the new changes as regards my present life. I began to wonder if these changes were just a dream or would I soon wake up to reality and face the nightmares of the past.

The troops and officers showed much concern about my welfare and made me feel very welcome. As for Jim, he just couldn't do enough for me and made sure I was being taken care of as regards to my daily needs. They even gave me a small dog for a Christmas present. They told me the dog was my mascot and I was their mascot.

Meanwhile as the days went past, the battles from the Civil war continued. Most of the bedroom windows of the Hotel, were protected with sandbags and machine guns. By the third week of December, 1944, the firing around Omonia had increased. One day during that week I felt well enough and started to increase my activity around the hotel, in order to exercise my little dog that was given to me for Christmas by the army. When I reached the ground floor over the reception door I let my little dog run around the hall not realising at the time that the front door of the hotel, was open and guarded by the British military guards outside.

Those guards had orders never to leave their posts under any circumstances. Suddenly, my little dog which I had come to love and treasure ran out onto the road and was now around Omonia Square directly opposite to the

Hotel. The guards outside were calling the dog to come back. It was then when I realised that my dog whose name was Little, ran out of the hotel. Without hesitation I ran out of the Hotel, and made for the square opposite forgetting in the meantime the dangers that confronted me with all the shooting around the area. I somehow became more concerned for his safety than mine. The guards outside the hotel, and those guarding the hotel with machine guns from the bedroom windows above were shouting for me to come back or I would be killed.

I was determined to save him and soon managed to pick him up. Crossing the road in the general direction of the Hotel, I held him in my arms. Suddenly a bullet hit Little my dog. I became hysterical and started to run toward the entrance of the hotel. No one seemed to know at the time which direction the bullet was fired from as there were snipers all over the place.

In the meantime as I placed Little, my dog on the steps at the entrance of the hotel I tried to get some response from him while tears were pouring down my face. One of the guards pulled me up and said "Come on Titch, Little is dead, you are lucky it could have been you."

Just then Jim came and took me inside. He told me to put on my other uniform as the one I had on was now

185

badly stained with blood. He said this uniform would now have to be thrown out but we will make you new ones when the fighting ends. A few days later on Christmas day I was taken by Jim and the staff sergeant to the NAFI next door to the hotel, occupied by the British troops to have our Christmas lunch. Ten minutes or so later as we were about to start our Christmas feast along with many of the troops and officers, someone from the building across the street started to spray his machine gun through the NAFI's large windows. Most of us had just managed to take cover under the table whilst the food and dishes above us fell all over the place.

Luckily no-one was killed but a couple of soldiers received minor injuries. Just then there was a return burst of machine gun fire by a British soldier from one of the hotel's bedroom above us and the sniper was shot down almost immediately. Although it spoiled our Christmas feast, later we celebrated the remainder of the Christmas in the hotel.

After Christmas the fighting had increased, and the streets of Athens were completely deserted for many weeks. The only life to be seen was from all those involved in the bitter fighting.

I would often hang around by the front door of the hotel, between the two guards, and sometimes I would chat with some of the Greek police while they took cover by the hotel. I could hear them complaining amongst each other as regards to the poor weapons they had to fight with. One of them said, "If only we had powerful rifles like the British."

One day as I stood by the reception desk with nothing to do, one of the soldiers tapped me on the back and said, "Hello, Titch, would you like to help me fill the oil lamps on the platforms at the railway just outside." "OK." I said. I didn't know the soldier's name at the time as there were too many troops to remember them all. As he was filling the oil lamps, the shooting came closer to home and he was forced to abandon what he came down to do and take cover. He told me at the time to take cover behind him. Seconds later we heard noises further down the railway track. He then shouted, "Who goes there?" In return we received a burst of rifle fire. The British soldier with me, gave them a burst of machine-gun fire and told me to go back to the hotel and get help. While the shooting continued I started to crawl on my hands and knees to the general direction of the railway steps leading to the hotel outside, when he cried out from pain as he received a bullet in the shoulder.

At that moment I turned back and went to his aid. By the time I got to him he was losing a lot of blood. I took off my shirt and told him to hold it by his wound to lessen the loss of blood. I then snatched his machine-gun and tried to fire it along the railway track but the magazine was by now empty. He told me to put it down before I hurt myself. I told him that I knew how to fire it, I had fired once before on the Germans. "Give me your spare magazine to reload this one is empty" I said to him. By now the bullets were bouncing closer to home. When I finally changed the magazine I told him, that I was going to fire a few rounds down the railtrack in order to buy us time for me to help him get to the steps of the railway. From there we would be able to get help from the troops above. I had to practically drag him backwards with the help of his left hand.

We stopped for a moment and I went back and fired another round down the dark hall of the railway track to let them know whoever was firing at the other end that we were still here in order to give us a little more time to reach the steps. Eventually after a little struggle we made it. I then ran up the steps to the entrance and raised the alarm.

Afterwards I rushed back to comfort him and told him help was on the way. By that time he was too dazed to take much notice of what I was saying to him. Within seconds afterwards troops from the hotel rushed down

An artist's impression
how Titch helped a British soldier to safety when he was wounded during an attack at the railway underground in Omonia, Athens at the hart of the civil war December 1944.

by Alan Morgan

the steps with a stretcher and from there on they took over. Within a minute or so later he was brought up to the hotel entrance, the army red cross ambulance came from nearby and he was taken away.

Afterwards the commanding officer took the machine-gun from around my shoulder and rubbed his hand on my head. He told me to go to my room and put on another shirt. Half an hour or so later Jim came to my room and said, "Come on Titch. The Captain wants to see us in his office. When we entered his office the interpreter was also there. At that moment I felt the shivers of fear inside me. I thought I had done something wrong and they were going to send me away.

When we entered his office he told us to take a seat. The Captain then translated his questions to me through the interpreter. Since the soldier that got wounded was taken to hospital, he wanted me to brief him about what happened down there and what was I doing down the railway in the first place. After I explained everything and the reasons I was there, he said, "Where did you learn to shoot?"

I told him sometime back I got involved with the Resistance for a short period of time by accident, and they taught me about guns and grenades during the time I spent with them on the mountain. I had no parents - no home, and had been running from the Germans to avoid execution for some time now. I had been sleeping amongst the ruins of Piraeus and The Acropolis.

As he kept firing his questions at me I started to cry and said, "I don't want to talk any more of the past, please don't make me." "Very well, Titch." came his reply, "No more questions. No crying." he said to me, "you are a soldier now, soldiers don't cry do they?"

He then said, "I think you are a brave little lad." while Jim wiped the tears from my eyes with his handkerchief. The Captain gave me a large bar of chocolate and told Jim to take me to the mess and gave me some tea and cakes.

As the days went by the fighting in Athens got much worse and every now and then the shooting was coming closer to home. The army would often bring out one of their tanks from next door and fire shells and heavy machine-gun fire at the enemy down the long road from Omonia by the side of the hotel. One day I was standing at the door of the hotel between the two guards trying to understand what they were saying to me as my English was not too good at that time. Just then we heard shooting just down the road. As I looked to my right I saw one Greek policemen at the street opposite across the next block from where we were, struggling to get to his feet after he was shot down. To get to him, one had to cross the long road to the right of the hotel. To do that it would have been suicidal without the protection of a tank. This I didn't know at the time and made a quick dash to try and help him.

In the meantime the guards at the door of the hotel, were calling for me to come back. As I tried to cross to the street opposite in order to help the wounded policeman, I was being fired at with machine-gun by the enemy from the long road to my right. Halfway across, I was forced to make a dive and lay flat on the ground. The bullets were now zipping past missing me by an inch or two.

Two British soldiers with machine-guns came to my aid at the corner of the hotel, but could not reach me due to the heavy fire. One of them shouted at me and told me to stay where I was and not to move as help was on the way.

Within seconds a tank was brought out from next door to the hotel, and was driven to where I was lying. He stopped dead centre from where I was and fired several shells and heavy machine-gun fire down the long road.

In the meantime, the two soldiers at the corner of the hotel, dashed to the back of the tank and I was dragged out backwards from under the tank. Whilst the tank continued to fire up the road, one of them helped me to cross the road in the general direction of the hotel. The other soldier went to the aid of the wounded policeman. Moments later the wounded policeman was rescued and was taken away by an army ambulance. Some time later I was approached by the Captain with the interpreter at his side and said, "I know you mean well at heart, but you must not run out into the street like that unprotected, you could have been killed along with others trying to rescue you." He made me promise that in future I must not leave the hotel on my own unless I was accompanied by the troops. He then smiled and said, "You might think you have more than one life, but that's no reason to take advantage of it." As the fighting got much worse I was confined to the boundaries of the hotel, and sometimes next door where all the Army's vehicles and tanks were kept. During this time I had time to take stock of my situation. As I kept looking in the mirror, I could see that my uniform which I admired very much at the time was beginning to take a better shape around my body. Just like Jim said it would in time. Even my face was beginning to show an enormous improvement thanks to the army.

The next morning during breakfast, Jim said "Titch, how would you like to go with us for a ride in the tank." "Oh, yes please Jim." I said. Two of Jim's mates then said to me "Be downstairs by the door in half an hour." A patrol was organised to go on a mission to another British camp several miles away.

The patrol consisted of 4 soldiers in a small truck armed to the teeth escorted by the tank Jim and I were in. At that moment for me to ride inside a tank was indeed a thrilling experience.

During our journey all the streets were completely deserted except for the outburst of fire some distance away. After several miles the tank turned into a side street and screeched to a halt.

Jim told me to stay put inside the tank whilst he went out to attend to something. A moment or so later large doors of some kind of a warehouse building were forced open by the force of the tank. The tank backed away and the area was guarded for a while with an extra machine gun from above the tank. Moments later Jim called for me to come out for a moment. He helped me down from the tank and said, "Come and see what the Germans have left behind." When I walked in and saw what was in there my eyes practically lit up.

He then said, "It looks as if the Germans were preparing for a much longer stay." Jim told me to help myself to anything I wanted. I picked up several things such as shoes, socks, pyjamas, underwear and handkerchiefs. "Don't worry if they don't fit you." he said. "After the war we will have them cut down to your size." As my eyes wandered around I could see several five gallon tins of assorted sweets and many thousand packs of cigarettes.

I helped them to load some of the goods on to the vehicle outside. Later I said to Jim, "After the war I can sell a lot of these things on the black market and make a lot of money for you." Jim smiled and said, "We will see, Titch."

When we finished loading I was lifted back onto the tank. We then travelled several more miles and eventually arrived in another British Army camp. There must have been about a thousand or more troops there. When Jim helped me out of the tank many of the troops around seemed to be very much surprised at my presence there. I then realised that my age and uniform were attracting a lot of attention amongst the troops. We had lunch there and in the afternoon made our way back to Athens. During our journey we came under attack from rifle snipers. The tank then screeched to a halt. In the meantime the truck and troops in it took cover at the side of the tank whilst it continued to fire several shells down the road and later a burst of heavy machine-gun fire.

After a short delay we eventually made our way back to Omonia Square. By now I became very attached to the troops and in many ways they just couldn't do enough for me. Jim however had been responsible for my welfare throughout the Civil war and by the time the fighting came to an end in Athens we became very close friends and attached to each other.

In the meantime, although my body was showing a tremendous improvement my mental state differed. Every now and then the nightmares of the past crowded in my mind making me forget the changes in my present life. This, however, now and then made me behave a little strangely as fear and confusion started to creep inside me.

Jim had experienced these changes of my mental problems on several occasions and at one stage became very concerned. One day he started to shake my shoulders in order to wake me from my nightmares of the past. Although the Civil war continued in the midst until 1949, by the third week of January 1945, the bitter fighting in Athens and Piraeus was brought to an end.

Soon after as near as February 1945, life started to function on the streets once again. Law and order was beginning to be restored. Makeshift schools started to open up. Cinemas and public transport began to operate. Even the black market started to thrive like never before.

Soon afterwards the bright lights throughout the

capital began to shine again. Night life started tofunction as forces from other nations started to arrive.

In the meantime Jim and some of the troops said to
me, now that the fighting is over how would I like to do
something for them and for myself. "I will Jim." said I.

They asked me if I was familiar with the black market.
"Oh, yes." I replied. They took me next door to the hotel
where all the army vehicles were kept and showed me all
the goods they wanted me to sell off.

They said it's only a few things the Germans have left
behind. They told me that they will provide me with
transport and I will be given plain clothes to wear during
the sale not to attract any attention.

We all agreed and made a start the next day. It took
me about four days to sell off most of the goods on the
black market and we made a lot of money.

Suddenly it all came to a halt and the next day I was
asked to go with Jim to the Captain's office. I sensed
then that something was wrong and fear started to creep
inside me. During my time spent with the British army I
had found security and happiness like never before.

However, the thought often entered my mind at the
time as to what would happen to me when the war came
to an end. Meanwhile as we entered the Captain's office
and saw the interpreter there, almost immediately I

sensed that something was wrong.

The thought that they may send me away entered my mind and I started to shiver like a leaf. The Captain explained to me through the interpreter that he and the troops have had orders to leave Athens for the time being as they were needed in Italy to fight the Germans.

In the meantime I have become a problem for them as they didn't know what to do with me. He told me, at the moment the country is in a mess and it is quite impossible to make proper provisions for me in such a short space of time.

However he said we have a couple of ideas but we want you to make your own choice in the matter. Number one, they could hand me over to the Greek police until such time as arrangements could be made for my welfare as soon as there was stability in the country.

Your other choice is, Jim knows a woman who lives across the road and we could give her a little money to take care of you until some of us came back here at a later date. "At least we will know where to find you." he said. I will go with the woman across the road I replied whilst tears ran down my face. Jim made arrangements straight away as they had orders to move out the next day. At this point of time I was heartbroken over this.

In the meantime Jim tried to comfort me by saying he

will come back for me whatever happens. He said we have given her a lot of money to take care of you until we return. The thought of them coming back for me and the money I made from the goods I sold on the black market did provide me at the time with a little comfort.

The house across the road

Chapter 13

**THE TROOPS DEPARTURE
AND REUNION**

The night before their departure I was introduced to the woman across the street and moved in to her place with a small bundle of my belongings. The next day after they left, I realised that I couldn't go about wearing my British army uniform so I wrapped it into a nice bundle and kept if for when they came back for me.

In the meanwhile I wore my civilian clothes to go out and about not to attract attention on the streets. By the next day I learnt that this woman who was about thirty seven to forty years of age, happened to be a prostitute. Her accommodation consisted of one room only and every time she brought a soldier up to her room for sex I was made to go out and walk the street. Very late one night she asked me to sleep under the bed as she was expecting a visitor and not to come out unless I was told to.

In many ways I wasn't very happy with her but in some ways it was better than sleeping on the streets again. However a few weeks later she said she didn't think that they were coming back for me and she could not afford to keep me any longer and to go and seek help with the police or wherever I could. By this time I felt that I had taken just about all I could from her and straight away I picked up my few belongings in a bundle and left.

I was now back on the streets of Athens once again. However I was now in better physical health than I was three months ago except for my confused state of mind. At least I now had shoes on my feet, clean clothes, and a little money that I made from the sale of goods on the black market. I took a walk in the general direction of Constitution Square for the first time since I was caught in the shooting on 3rd December 1944 at the start of the Civil War.

On my way there I stopped to buy some nuts from an old man off a barrel. During our conversation I asked him if he had a job to offer me. He said "Where do you live?" "Anywhere I can as I don't have a home." said I.

"Call back here tomorrow around the same time." he said, "and we can discuss it then." I went back the next day just like he told me too. He said his wife wasn't very well at the moment and he can do with a little help. He also said in the meantime I can stay in the house but I would have to sleep in the little shed just outside the house. As there was only one room in his little house, "I don't mind that." I replied. I was now very pleased at having some-where to sleep. In the meantime I had plans of my own.

I worked close to him for a few days in order to learn the trade. A week later he told me that his wife will not be able to help him with the business any more due to her illness. He said how would you like to have your own barrel and sell nuts. Oh yes please, I will sell a lot of nuts for you, you see I said to him. In the meantime I was working it all out. If I was given my own barrel I could go to Omonia Square and sell the nuts. That way I would be able to keep an eye on the area in case Jim and the troops came back for me.

I then said to the old man if I wait outside the cinema in Omonia Square I will sell a lot more nuts. Although at the time deep in my heart I knew that this wasn't the reason for me wanting to go to Omonia.

"OK." he said, "so long as I know where you are." At that moment of time I was very grateful to the old man for offering me a job and somewhere to sleep, but my heart was longing for Jim and the troops to come back for me. Late one night two weeks later I was across the street from the cinema in Omonia Square selling my nuts. Due to the music I had heard from the night-club below, I was encouraged by this to take a peep through the little window behind me. Suddenly much to my surprise I spotted Jim and some of the troops down there and they all appeared to be having a good time. At that moment I started to shiver from my excitement and moved my barrel close to the entrance of the night-club not for me to miss them when they came out.

When they eventually came out I then realised that they all had one drink too many. As I approached them, "Hello Jim." said I. "Titch." he shouted as he put his arms around me, "where have you been we have been looking everywhere for you." At this stage I couldn't control my emotions and tears started to run down my face. Due to one drink to many that they had, they were in no position to make a clear conversation and Jim told me to meet him the next morning at the palace officers mess just up the road on the left-hand side and to wear my uniform. He said to ask for him when I got there. That night I took the barrel of nuts back to the old man's house, gave him the money from the sale, had a bite to eat and then I tried to get some sleep.

In the meantime I didn't say anything to the old man until the next morning. That night I hardly slept due to my excitement and was up and about long before the old man and his wife.

I had a little wash from the little water tap in the yard just outside the shed where I slept and later I put on my smart uniform. When the old man woke up and saw me in my uniform his eyes nearly popped out. I never told him about my involvement with the British army during the civil war, and said to him I will explain everything to you some other time. I told him that I now had to go to the

Officer's mess and hopefully they will have me back. With that he said, "You are always welcome here you know that."

I thanked him for everything and started to make my way to the Officer's mess. On my way there I somehow felt a little secure in my mind knowing that there was a place for me to come back to should anything go wrong.

As I made my way there I seemed to have attracted a lot of attention on the streets in view of my uniform. When I eventually arrived at the Officer's mess I told the guard outside that I had come to see Jim. "You are Titch." he said, "Yes." I replied. It appeared to me at the time that everyone had heard of me prior to my arrival there.

Suddenly Jim arrived at the entrance. He put his arms around me and later introduced me to the guard at the door. He then escorted me inside and I was introduced to everyone in the canteen and the sergeant in charge of the kitchen.

Jim gave me a cold drink and told me to sit here for a while whilst he went to attend to something. A few moments later several soldiers that were with me and Jim at the hotel in Omonia Square during the fighting, walked in for coffee, not realising at first that I was there sat in the corner with my cold drink. When they finally spotted me they practically hit the roof from their excitement.

They then came and sat by me and with my little English and their broken Greek we had managed to communicate a little. Later the sergeant in charge of the kitchen came and joined us bringing with him a big dish of hot donuts. "Tuck in Titch." said the sergeant I hadn't been there an hour and everyone was treating me as if I was someone special.

I was so overwhelmed from all the concern and attention I was given by everyone, I kept saying to myself I hope I am not dreaming all this. A little while later Jim came back for me and said "Come on then Titch, Captain Rowland who is the Commanding Officer is longing to meet you. He said you don't have to be nervous as he knows all about you." He told me that he was a very nice man and also a very good friend of his.

When we entered Captain Rowland's office there were several other people there. A Greek interpreter, Lieutenant Barnes, the Staff Sergeant, and another sergeant whose name was Vincent. After I met everyone, the language was translated to me through the interpreter. Captain Rowland then asked me where I had been sleeping since the troops left the hotel. He said "We know about the woman across the road from the hotel Jim left you with, what happened there?"

I explained to him that a few weeks after the troops

left, she said she couldn't afford to keep me any longer and didn't want me so I left. Afterwards I slept in a little shed outside an old man's house whilst I sold the nuts for him. "Well." he said, "from now on you will not be sleeping in any sheds or streets any more." He said, "Until such time when we know what provision we can make for you, you are now officially an adopted member of the British army. You will be accommodated along with the troops at the Majestic hotel just up the road from the military mess, and you will be provided with a room of your own. Sergeant Vincent and Jim will only be a few doors away should you need anything. In the meantime you will take your orders from them and me. As for your meals, you will eat here at the Officer's mess with the other troops.

A Greek tailor will be here tomorrow after breakfast to measure you for your new uniforms. On the sleeves of your new uniforms you will have three stripes which will make you the smallest sergeant in the British army. You will also be given documents to carry with you at all times in case you should at any time get stopped by the Greek police when you are out by yourself. You will also call upon the staff sergeant down in the store room to draw your weekly needs such as toothpaste, soap, haircream, white paste to clean your belt with, boot polish and some

"Titch" dressed in his tailord British uniform - Athens 1945.

Cpt. Rowland and "Titch" make theur way through the streets of Athens enroute for American army H/O - Athens 1945.

"Titch" poses on top of a British army truck bonnet in Athens 1945

Commanding officer capt. L.R. Rowland (second on left) poses with N.C.O.'s outside the officers mess in an Athens hotel during 1944.

"Titch" with capt. Rowland and Jim the officer who did so much to help "Titch" in the early stages of British army adoption as a mascot.

211

chocolate. Until you know your way around, for a couple of weeks you will be escorted everywhere. Sometimes by Jim, Sergeant Vincent, or my self. We will be your guardian from now on and you must obey orders for the benefit of your welfare. Do you think you can remember everything you have been told so far." he said. "I will sir." I replied.

I was also given a regular job every morning to go with one of the troops by truck to collect all the bread and cakes for the Officer's mess and the regiment at the Army barracks some six miles away. As the months of 1945 passed, Captain Rowland, Jim, Sergeant Vincent, and Lieutenant Barnes, they all have been like a father to me. They always treated me with a lot of respect and love, and in many ways I was spoilt.

By now I had become very attached to the regiment, and their concern for my welfare had grown to a very high level. Sometimes we would spend the afternoons sunbathing on the roof of the hotel, and in the evening Sergeant Vincent, Jim and some of the troops would take me out to the night life of Athens. Sometimes to a cinema, a danceclub, or to a night-club. Most of the time everywhere they went I went.

Sometimes I would have dinner with Captain Rowland and other high rank officers in the Officer's mess. In view of all this, I had to be very clean at all times. Due to my smart sergeant's uniform and my age I appeared to have attracted a lot of attention on the streets and wherever we went. Captain Rowland would often walk me around to show me off to other officer's during their meal at the Officer's mess. At this stage of my life I don't remember at any other time ever having so much happiness. Everyone would give me things including money. Apart from all that, it was all the kindness, love, care and attention I have had from everyone at the time that had provided me with so much happiness.

Although at this point of time I was painting a rosy and happy picture of my present life, my future was in the balance. In the meantime the fear was always on my mind that the day will come when I will be abandoned once again when the army evacuate from Greece and the good life and happiness will all crumble around me like a pack of cards once again. By this time although there was tremendous improvement in my English language, it was unintelligible for making conversation or to answer questions but, I did manage to get by with odd words.

Then one day in July 1945, I was told to go to Captain Rowland's office with the Greek interpreter, Jim, and Sergeant Vincent. When we finally entered his office he translated enormous amounts of questions to me through the interpreter as regards to my parents my home and my age. I don't know my age I replied and my parents died from starvation. I told him of my involvement with the resistance for a short time by accident and a little about my escapes from the Germans and also of having to sleep rough with hardly any food inside the ruined buildings of Piraeus.

I could not tell him about my home in Kokkinia now called Nikaia as they would have taken me there and back to Evangelos so I told him my home was bombed in Piraeus. By this time I broke down with tears running down my face and told the Captain I don't want to talk about my past any more and begged him not to force me into answering any questions. At this moment he put his arms around me and said, "Very well Titch, no more questions but tomorrow morning we will go to Piraeus and see if we can find any records of your birth certificate. We need to know your age don't we?" he said. The next day Jim drove Captain Rowland and me to Piraeus in an open jeep to see if they could find my birth certificate but to no avail.

Some time later whilst we had some coffee and donuts in a near by British army NAAFI the Captain said that the Germans must have destroyed most of the records. A month or so later Captain Rowland, Jim, and the interpreter sat with me during a coffee break and tried to explain to me that they could be ordered back to England at any time at short notice. He said "In the meantime we want to make some kind of provisions for you otherwise you might end up on the streets again after we have gone. You understand what we are saying don't you." he said. "Can I come to England with you." I said to him.

"That would be very difficult to organise from here." he said. "Tomorrow we will go to the Greek authority and see if there is anything they can do to help." That day must have been the most unhappiest of my life for me for a long time. Whilst I continued with my duties in the mess, some of the troops must have noticed this, as it was showing on my face and one of them said, "Cheer up Titch, it's not the end of the world." "It is for me." I replied

That night as much as I tried not to think of the next day, it became impossible not to do so. My heart seemed to have cracked inside me making it difficult for me to breathe. As I realised at the time how much Captain Rowland, Jim and all those close to me in the Officer's mess meant to me, the thought of not being with them much longer was tearing my heart apart.

My life throughout the war had been distracted so much from one day to the next I now felt that I couldn't take any more. At this stage I had found so much love and happiness with the troops, Jim, and Captain Rowland that I somehow just couldn't come to terms with the thought that it will soon be all over. The instability of my present and future life was tearing me apart inside and as I found it difficult to sleep that night, I opened my bedroom window in the middle of the night with the thought in mind of doing away with my life by throwing myself over the balcony. After a great deal of thought my confidence returned which soon discharged the idea from my mind.

The next day after breakfast, Captain Rowland, Jim and the interpreter took me for a ride in the jeep and afterwards we stopped for refreshments at an army NAAFI. Some time later when we got back into the jeep I was driven to the main police station in Athens. Inside whilst Captain Rowland was having his conversation translated to the chief of police about my future, my heart was beating at an erratic pace from fear that they were going to leave me there.

Some time later I was asked to wait with Jim in the other room for a few moments. I realised then that they were discussing my future behind closed doors. A while later we were called back into the office. I was then told that the police officer will arrange for me to be taken to a home where they kept many other homeless children and there I would be able to attend to my education.

Jim said he will bring my belongings from the hotel in a day or so. At that moment the thought of having to part from Captain Rowland and Jim it was as if someone stuck a knife in my heart. After they said goodbye to me and started to walk towards the jeep outside the station I just couldn't contain my feelings for them and ran out of the building crying my heart out as I put my arms around Captain Rowland's waist and begged him not to leave me there and to take me back with them.

At that moment everyone's emotions were running so high even Jim was showing a few tears. Captain Rowland then said, "Come on Titch you coming back with us even if I have to adopt you myself." As we drove back to the officer's mess that day I was still trembling a little, but now more so from happiness than fear. Until that very emotional day at the police station, I don't think any of us realised before just how we felt about each other.

When we arrived at the officer's mess the few troops that were there at the time learned from Jim that Captain Rowland changed his mind and I will be staying here until such time when arrangements were made for me to go to England, and for the time being it was to be kept quiet. In the meantime the good news about my stay at the mess brought many cheers from the troops, who even arranged a small welcome back party for me the following night with a gift of a lovely watch from everyone.

At this stage I was not aware of my going to England until many weeks later. In the meantime Captain Rowland didn't waste any time in making arrangement for my future life and many things I didn't understand at the time had began to happen around me.

Photographs were being taken of me on the streets and behind closed doors by the Americans and the British. Some of the photographs taken of me at the time I wasn't aware of. One day Captain Rowland introduced me to a high rank American lady officer, and later Captain Rowland and I were driven in her jeep by her driver to her headquarters in Constitution Square opposite the palace in Athens.

Inside we were escorted to a room on the next floor and was first photographed on my own and later the three of us together. Even up to this stage I had no knowledge as to what was going on or the reason for all the photographs. Some time later we had lunch at the American officer's mess below.

In the meantime I was told nothing of what they had in mind as regards to my future. Some time later a Greek lady in her 30's who was well educated in the English language was brought to the officer's mess to work with the administration staff. Her name happened to be Evthoxia. The same name as the resistance girl I was with on the mountain not so long ago. Captain Rowland then arranged her hours in order to provide me with a few hours a day three days a week to educate me in the English language.

During this time, as the weeks went by I was having a lovely time. Sometimes on weekends Captain Rowland, Jim, and Sergeant Vincent would take me to the seaside at the Faliro and teach me how to swim. A couple of times Captain Rowland and I were taken out to tea some distance away by the American lady officer in her jeep. At night I would go with Jim and some of the troops and explore the night life in Athens, and on one specific occasion I got drunk and had to be carried back to our hotel.

Then one day towards the end of the summer 1945 things had begun to happen. Jim said, "Come on Titch, Captain Rowland and his guests are waiting to see us at the other end of the mess room." On our arrival at Captain's Rowland's table I was confronted by a group of people including the American lady officer I met on several occasions.

Whilst they were all having their morning coffee, a lot of discussion was going on amongst them as regards to my future. Some time later I was shown photographs of myself with Captain Rowland and the American lady officer in newspapers and in an American magazine. They then said, "We have some good news for you. You have a chance to go to England or to United States. The choice is yours. You can have a little time to think about it if you like." - I thought about my sister with sadness, but Evangelos was there and I feared him. I made my decision. I gave them my answer. "I'd like to go to England with Captain Rowland and Jim." I replied.

Captain Rowland said, "Since we don't know your age as we have been unable to find any records we will have to give you an adopted one. Your adopted date of birth will be from now on 13th December 1932. In the meantime we are going to arrange a passport for you." - I was officially 13 years old.

For a month or so my life at the officer's mess went on as usual and I continued to receive my English education from Evthoxia preparing me for when the day came to go to England and a new life. In the meantime the Captain was arranging my passport and other papers from the Home Office in England to my entering Great Britain.

It appeared I was bound for a place called South Wales in Britain which was a principality attached to England.

Chapter 14

THE ARRIVAL OF TITCH INTO BRITAIN

Cardiff Officer "Adopts" Greek War Orphan

"TITCH," a ten-year-old Athens boy, who lost in one blow his entire family, is learning to live again—thanks to the good deed of a Cardiff-born officer, Captain Llewellyn Rowland, serving in Greece with The Welch Regiment.

A year ago, the little Greek orphan was a ragged, cold, hungry, desolate child who had endured the long misery of German occupation.

To-day he is sturdy, healthy and happy, and proudly wears the uniform of a British sergeant.

The work of U.N.R.R.A. has, of course, done as much for many thousands of Greek children. But the story of Tich is unique, since he is an "adopted" member of a British military mess and is the special protege of Capt. Rowland.

He wandered into the mess 12 months ago, when street fighting raged in Athens. There he was fed, warmed and comforted. Shirts and slacks were cut down to fit him, and soon he put up his three stripes. He lost his expression of fear, of defensiveness, of nervous tension. He began his schooling—he began to laugh.

Now, Capt. Rowland is looking for a home which will adopt the "sergeant" permanently, and continue the good work. A year has done a lot for Tich; care, affection and the resources of U.N.R.R.A. have given him a fresh chance.

Captain Rowland, who is 34, is the second son of Lady Rowland, 103, Cathedral-road, Cardiff, and of the late Sir John Rowland, chairman of the Welsh Board of Health. He was educated at Cardiff High School for Boys and played Rugby for the school and also in the Cardiff second team. He is married and his wife lives at 52, Heathwood-road, Cardiff.

1945

O ne morning a week or so later a letter arrived
for me at the officer's mess from Wales.
Before I had a chance to open it, Captain
Rowland, Lieutenant Barnes, Sergeant Vincent, Jim,
and the interpreter sat around me during morning coffee
break and gave me all the good news as regards my
future. At this stage I didn't have a clue as to who sent
me the letter, but all the information was revealed to me
during this time as we were all having our coffee.

Whilst Captain Rowland translated all the good news
to me through the interpreter, he first said, "There is a
family in South Wales who want to adopt you and bring
you up as their own." At that moment I interrupted him
and said "Will you be very far away from where I am
going?" I was overwhelmed when he said that his house
was only half an hour drive to where I would be going
and that he would visit me quite often and take me out
to tea with his wife. He said he had been ordered back to
England and he was due to leave in a month's time. He
told me that after his departure from Greece Lieutenant
Barnes will be in charge of the officer's mess and will
deal with all the necessary details as regards to my flight
to England as soon as all the arrangements had been
made.

"Sergeant Vincent and Jim will be your daily

guardians. Should you have any problems you discuss them with Lieutenant Barnes. The letter you have received this morning was from Mr and Mrs Rowland your future adopted parents in Wales. They just happen to have the same name as me." I then opened the envelope and the interpreter read the letter to me in Greek. Inside there was also a five pound note. Just then Captain Rowland said, "That's a lot of money Titch, you ought to put it in a safe place until you go to England."

A few weeks later on the day the Captain was about to depart from Greece for South Wales, I just couldn't control my tears. He then said, "Come on now Titch, no tears you will soon be coming to South Wales and we will then be near each other." In the meantime whilst I waited to fly to Britain and to my new life during the long remaining months of 1946, the thought of meeting with Captain Rowland and my new adopted parents did provide me with a lot of comfort, happiness and much excitement.

During those waiting months of 1946, Jim was now ordered back to England and I was being looked after by Sergeant Vincent and Evthoxia who was educating me in the English language. Lieutenant Barnes was also very good to me and every now and then would take me for a drive in the jeep. During this time Sergeant Vincent and

Evthoxia's relationship had grown and I believe they got married sometime after I arrived in England.

Fifty years on up to this day I have never heard or seen them since, and the same applies to Jim. In the meantime whilst I waited for the day to be told to board the plane for Britain, I spent most of my time with Sergeant Vincent and Evthoxia going to the seaside swimming, picnic trips, and long drives in the jeep. During this time I received many letters from my future parents and Captain Rowland saying we are all anxiously waiting for your arrival in South Wales.

Then one evening during the first week of October 1946, I got all dressed up in my smart uniform for a night out in Athens with a couple of the troops and Sergeant Vincent. I was told to meet them all at the officer's mess. When I arrived there I was confronted by Sergeant Vincent, Evthoxia, Lieutenant Barnes, and almost all the troops that were involved with the officer's mess celebrating the good news of my flight to Britain. At this stage I thought they were celebrating someone's birthday. Suddenly Lieutenant Barnes broke the good news to me and said that I will be flying to England next week. For a moment I just stood there trembling from all the excitement. I was then given a small glass of beer and a sandwich and they all wished me the very best of luck with my new life and parents in South Wales. Just then I couldn't control my emotions and a few happy tears started to run down my face. An hour or so later the celebrations ended and I was then taken by Sergeant Vincent and two other soldiers to celebrate the remainder of the night in one of the night clubs in Athens. During my last week at the officer's mess Lieutenant Barnes, Sergeant Vincent and Evthoxia began to prepare me for my long journey to Britain. They even had an army rucksack cut down to my size so that I would carry my belongings on my back like the troops did.

The night before I was to fly to Britain, as much as I tried to sleep I just couldn't and stayed awake most of the night awaiting daylight. During those long waiting hours my thoughts went back to those nightmare events of the war and for a while I just couldn't wait to get on the aeroplane for England.

At this stage of my life I somehow felt as if I was going to a new world to be reborn. The next morning never came too soon for me. I had a good breakfast in the officer's mess and later I was briefed by Lieutenant Barnes how I was to get to South Wales when I got to London.

My instructions were that when the plane arrived in

England I was to board the coach from the airport to London. At the end of my coach journey I was to meet up with a married couple. He said I won't know them but they will know me from my uniform. I was to sleep at their house in London that night and the next day they will put me on the train at Victoria station for Newport South Wales. I was to wait at Newport platform until I was met by Captain Rowland and his wife along with my new adopted parents from a small town named Bargoed.

In the meantime everyone at the officer's mess came out to see me off. A few of them couldn't resist their emotions and one or two tears were showing amongst them as they all wished me good luck whilst I was about to be driven off in a jeep to the airport by Sergeant Vincent and Lieutenant Barnes. This was a very emotional moment for all of us that day and I should never forget it so long as I live. When we arrived at the airport I was given a hug by Lieutenant Barnes and Sergeant Vincent and said that they will come and visit me one day when they return to Britain. At that point of time this was the happiest day of my life. I had so much to look forward to that my mind was filled with excitement.

Flying in an aeroplane for the first time in my life was indeed a thrilling experience in those days. Apart from myself there was no more than a dozen people flying with me. We arrived in Britain some three days later. The plane wasn't up to standard which was to be expected due to the war, and had to make an emergency landing in Italy for repairs. We were then delayed there for two days before we were given the all clear to board the aircraft. After that ordeal we had a short break in France and eventually made it to Britain.

Throughout the journey, due to my age and my smart Sergeant's uniform I was attracting a lot of attention everywhere I went as many people at the time were very puzzled at what they were seeing. When I arrived in London there was no one there to meet. Whilst I stood at the pavement with my army rucksack on my back, the passing crowd just couldn't take their eyes off me. To some people I must have looked like a grown up soldier returning home at the end of the war. The only difference was that they couldn't make out whether they were seeing a twelve year old in my uniform or a twenty year old who looked very young for his age.

After having to wait for an hour or so I began to worry a little in case I was left stranded in a strange country. Suddenly a middle aged couple tapped me on the shoulder from behind and said, "I believe you are "Titch" from Athens." Yes." I replied. They then took me on a double decker bus to see the sights of London and afterwards we went to their house for dinner.

Later they told me that tomorrow they will put me on the train at Victoria station for South Wales. The next day they gave me a good breakfast and then they took me to Victoria by taxi where I got on the train.

When I arrived I was then met with Captain Rowland and his wife and also my new adopted parents. After a few hugs and handshakes they took me to the platform tea-room where we had tea and cakes before I was driven by Captain Rowland and his wife to my new home and a new life in Bargoed. By now it was getting a little late and the Captain and his wife were about to return to their home in Cardiff some twenty miles away. He then said he will call on me in a week's time to see how I was getting on. After they left, my new parents prepared me for a nice bath and afterwards they provided me with a new pair of pyjamas, a dressing gown, and a nice pair of slippers. Later we all had some supper, a little chat, and then a good night's sleep in the most comfortable bed I have ever slept on.

After sleeping rough in German cells and amongst the ruined buildings of Piraeus along with all the dangers that confronted me throughout the war this was indeed a treat. Whilst my adopted father had his Opticians shop to run, my adopted mother took me shopping for a whole week and bought me new clothes.

In the meantime I found it difficult to part with my army uniform as it was very sentimental to me. It reminded me a lot of the good times I had with the troops and the officer's mess. After all if it wasn't for the army I probably wouldn't be here now and most likely be dead. She said I must now try and put all the past behind me, and with their help I might learn to live a new life. At that time that was easier said than done. A month or so later they had to throw away everything I brought to England with me including my army uniforms in order to terminate some of the ugly memories of the war out of my mind. On several occasions I started to scream in my sleep and this kept my parents awake half of the night.

One night they caught me sleepwalking in my room. When they asked me what I was doing out of bed I said, "I can't find my gun, where is my gun." For a moment they didn't realise I was talking in my sleep, when they became aware of the situation they managed to get me back into bed. In the meantime my adopted parents did all they could for me at the time and provided me with almost everything I wanted including their name. They were very good to me in many ways but, what they often failed to understand was that I was not like other boys in

England in view of the disruption of my childhood life throughout the war and what I have gone through. Although I must confess, until now no one at the time really had much clear knowledge of my experiences of the war as I kept them locked inside me.

After two years or so at Bargoed school I had chosen to go into catering for two reasons. One, was to be close to food and the other due to the little experience I had gained at the officer's mess in Athens. My parents helped me tremendously at this stage and had managed to get me into the Savoy Hotel in London to gain some experience for my future career.

In 1950 my adopted parents had decided to go and live in St. Ives Cornwall due to my father's health. In 1955 he died and from then on my mother decided to live on her own apart from my occasional visit home when I got the chance.

In the meantime, fifty years on and the nightmares of my childhood life are still with me. Throughout my fifty years in Britain I have never been back to Greece or been on an aeroplane. During these fifty years I have thought many times of going back to Athens one day if only to find out if my sister and brother were still alive. But the fear has always been with me as to what level it would affect my mind should I be confronted with the memories of those nightmare times of the occupation and coming face to face with Evangelos.

In 1978 I decided to write my life story. In 1979 I found it difficult to complete parts of my book as at this stage it involved names and dates of incidents in Athens. In the meantime my book came to a temporary standstill whilst I tried to trace Captain Rowland. After a brief write up in the local newspaper they managed to trace his whereabouts. A few days later we were reunited. This was a very emotional day for both of us. At this stage we had so much to talk about I had to do several trips to his house in Cwmbran. His presence at this point of time brought me close to many memories of those war times I had tried to forget throughout the years. He agreed to help me with the book and we started to make good progress. As time went on he became very ill and later he died. I then abandoned the book to take a catering position in Cornwall to be near my 86 year old adoptive mother in case she needed me.

In 1982 I was contacted by the authorities in my place of work forty miles away in regards to my adopted mother's welfare. They said she was now bedridden and was unable to look after herself. They told me if I couldn't make any arrangements for her she would then have to go into an old people's nursing home. In the meantime I took the rest of the day off work and drove forty miles to St. Ives to see her.

When I entered the house from the back door she was so happy to see me she started to cry and kept saying, "Don't let them put me into an old people's home, promise me you won't let them." I told her, "No-one is going to put her in any home while I am alive. Would you like me to come home and look after you?" said I. "Would you." she said, "after all, you are all I have left in this world."

At that moment I too started to show a few tears as it reminded me of that very emotional day in 1945 when Captain Rowland was about to abandon me at the police station in Athens and later decided he just couldn't do it and said "Come on Titch you are coming back with us even if I have to adopt you myself."

I then gave up my catering career at the age of forty nine and continued to care for her for seven years 24 hours a day. By the end of the seven years my health started to deteriorate due to the pressures, stress, and loss of sleep. I came close to a nervous breakdown on two occasions. I was determined to make her see her hundredth birthday but it was not to be.

In 1989 she failed to survive an operation from a hip replacement and died in hospital at the age of ninety

233

four. Although she was only my adopted mother I couldn't have loved her any more if she was my real mother.

After her death it took me two years to get over it. In 1994 I decided to return to Cardiff in order to be close to old friends. I was now becoming anxious to trace the whereabouts of my sister Demitra and my half brother Evangelos should they have survived. It had taken many years for me to take the courage to return to all of those bad memories.

Then one day with my friends help we decided to contact the Red Cross in Athens to see if they might be of some help in tracing them. We waited many months with the hope of some news but to no avail. In the meantime with the help of a friend as companion I found the courage to return to Athens for the first time in fifty years with the hope of finding the house I lived in with my parents and sister if the Germans hadn't burnt it down like they did with many other villages. I was hoping from there I might learn of my sister's whereabouts should she still be alive. I was now with my friend on the plane from London to Athens.

The date of this trip was 14th May 1995. At this stage for me it was a daunting experience of returning to my birthland after fifty years, but I was also a little frightened of not knowing what I might find or what affects it would have upon me as regards to those nightmare times of the occupation. I was also a little frightened of going on an aeroplane as this was my first time on an aircraft since I came to Britain fifty years ago.

Due to the problems the plane had when I first came to England in 1946, I suppose that was a good enough reason to make me a little nervous. After we arrived at our hotel near Omonia square in Athens, later in the afternoon we had decided to explore the sights around Omonia, the Placka, Constitution Square, and the Acropolis. When my eyes glanced around Omonia and the hotel across the road from the square where I was stationed with the British troops during the Civil war at the end of 1944, all my war experiences hit me as if it all happened yesterday.

After half a century I somehow felt I had never left. However at that moment of time having someone with me helped to overcome my problems. As we walked up the road towards Constitution square the first thing that came home to me was the day of panic 3rtd December 1944 at the start of the civil war when I along with crowds of people had to run for our lives as many dead and wounded covered the pavements. We only had a week there so we had to cover a lot of ground in such a short

Athens 1995.
"Titch" returns to Athens 50 years later and visits his hiding place in the acropolis.

"Titch" finds his old hiding place in the Acropolis, which since W.W.II has now been filled with cement.

Museum

*The museum dedicated to the men and women who were executed by the NAZI's
1944*

237

time. The next day we started our research. We first paid a visit to the Athens Red Cross with the hope of some good news as regards to my sister's whereabouts but to no avail.

We then decided to go further afield and went by taxi to Nikaia seven or so miles outside Athens hoping to find the house I lived in with my parents and sister. We got within two miles from where our house was but due to many of the old little pre-war houses being replaced by new large blocks of flats I was by now beginning to have my doubts where the house was and my sister ever having survived the rest of the war. During our research I was faced with communication problems due to my long separation from Greece. Fifty years on and I had almost forgotten my birth language.

As we continued our desperate efforts to find the house not knowing at this stage that we were only a couple of miles away, we came across an area that was very familiar to me. As we walked around the perimeter I realised that this was the place I was brought from Piraeus with many others to be executed in August of 1944. A museum to the resistance fighters is now built on this sacred ground, but it was a little difficult to recognise it straightaway due to the changes inside the grounds and also outside. The perimeter in 1944 was much larger than it is now. I then said to my companion friend we only have a few more days left before we go back to England so let's try and contact a local television station and see if they could help in any way to trace my sister's whereabouts should she be alive.

We then got into a taxi and told the driver to take us to one of the local TV stations. When we entered the Athens Sky Television studio we were approached by a very nice young lady TV producer named Mina Spiliotopou. Luckily for us she spoke very good English and this made it possible to communicate. After hearing my story in brief she showed willingness to help.

She decided to do a documentary film with the hope that this would bring some response as to the whereabouts of my parent's house and my sister Demitra should she still be alive. During the filming inside the perimeter of the blocco at Kokkinia now called Nikaia near Piraeus from where I escaped during the summer of 1944, I knew then that we were only two or three miles from my parent's house but with so many changes in the last fifty years and small pre-war houses being replaced by large blocks of flats our task wasn't going to be very easy.

Afterwards with the help of a few local people the camera crew and Mina Spiliotopou we tried desperately

Kokkinia, NR. Athens 1995.
"Titch" visits the memorial museum dedicated to the Greek Resistance fighters.
Built on the site where hundreds of men and women were executed by the
NAZI's in August 1944 and from where "Titch" escaped execution.

Inside the MEMORIAL MUSEUM wich displays hundreds of photographs of
the executed partisans.

Titch interviewed by SKY television, Athens in May 1995.
In the search for his sister.

Titch returns to Omonia in Athens fifty years later and his first visit The Neon
now a restaurant and the hotel next door where he spent his time with the British
troops during the Civil war

to find the house but to no avail. We were then told that the film will be shown on TV the following week. In the meantime we only had one more day left before boarding the plane back to Britain.

A few days after we arrived in England I received a telephone call from the TV presenter Miss Spiliotopou in regards to some news about my family. She said the T.V. documentary had been broadcast and had obtained information. They traced my parent's house and that my sister had died only four years ago and my step-brother Evangelos died in 1962.

After the war my sister married my brother Evangelos as they were not blood related due to different parents but I was blood related to both of them. During their marriage she had five children and they are now all between forty to forty five years of age. They are all married and have large families of their own. I was then told that I now have a family of about twenty six including an Uncle, my mother's brother.

Miss Spiliotopou then told me that she would get back to me in a day or so after she checks that the information of the family was correct and would let me have all their names and telephone numbers for me to contact them. The next day she phoned back and presented me with all their names and telephone numbers. She said due to my language problem, one of my niece's husband spoke a little English and this could be of some help to me to communicate.

At this stage this was a very exciting and emotional times for me. Moments later I started to phone all my family I had never met. They said that their mother, that's my sister, told them in their later years of my disappearance and that I was possibly killed by the Germans. The next day I made the arrangements for my trip to Athens. I had to wait about ten days before I could go. During those ten days I hardly slept due to my excitement but we kept in touch by phone almost every day.

When I eventually boarded the plane for Athens this was no doubt the most thrilling and happiest moment of my life. When I arrived at Athens airport they were all there with flowers and the television cameras from Sky TV waiting to meet me and take me to Nikaia several miles away and to the house where I lived with my parents and sister before and during the war.

It is very difficult to put into words how I felt when our search ended and I walked into my parent's house, the house I was forced to leave fifty three years ago. They all made me very welcome and I spent a little time with each family so as we could get to know one another a

The house in Kokkinia, from where Titch ran away after the death of his mother and father.

"Titch" and some of his family outside the house he left fifty years ago.

little better. They all lived within a few miles from each other and this made it possible. As I had forgotten most of my birth language I had a little difficulty in communicating sometimes but somehow we managed. We then celebrated my return after fifty three years in taverns and at home.

Later when I returned to Britain I somehow found it difficult to adjust back to my normal life and now I have decided to pay more regular visits there sometime in the future. Now that I have found my real birth certificate in Piraeus after all these years, officially I now have 2 birthdays two names and two nationalities, I could also have two passports.

My one regret from this story, is that I did not have the courage to have returned to Athens much earlier than I did - if I had returned earlier I would have been in time to meet my sister before she died in 1990/91. All I could do now was to place flowers on her grave and weep for us both, but I am sure, with her wonderful family around her over many years, they must have been great compensation for a brother who was lost in 1943 and who took far too long to overcome his fears of going back home to Greece and his sister Demitra.

THE NAZI INVASION OF GREECE - 1941

German parachutists descend on Greece

PYRAEUS, ATHENS IN RUINS - 1941

After stuka dive bomber attacks

THE STARVING CHILDREN OF GREECE - 1942/44

Malnutrition

It's a miracle I lived through it all

How a 12-year-old World War II Greek partisan, who faced a firing squad and was adopted by a company of the Welch Regiment, found a new identity in the Valleys

Wednesday, 25 September 1996

LIFE   The Western Mail 9

JOHN WILLIAMS

SEARED into the mind of Lyn Rowland is a hot dusty day in Greece in 1944 when, bedraggled, exhausted and just 12 years old, he was dragged in front of a firing squad by German soldiers.

Along with three men he was tied to a pole and blindfolded. He heard orders shouted, rifle bolts click and shots echo around the yard. He was unharmed, but the others were dead.

Leap forward half a century or so and Lyn, now 63, is living quietly in Cardiff.

He has written a book about his extraordinary childhood: how for three years he barely survived in and around war-ravaged Athens, became linked with partisans, killed Germans, was captured, escaped, captured again and nearly died in a notorious massacre. He still struggles with the trauma of that dreadful time.

"It was difficult to write the book," he said, as we talked at his Whitchurch home. "It made me remember things I would rather forget."

His story has two amazing twists.

Twist one came late in 1944 when, after Welch Regiment soldiers found the starving boy near to death at their Athens base, an officer got him adopted by a couple in Wales, which is how Elias Yiaïouris became a very Welsh-sounding Lyn Rowland.

Twist two came just last year when for the first time in 50 years he returned to Greece and confront his traumatic past. He always thought his family would be untraceable, but by chance uncovered many relatives, who were dumbfounded by his sudden appearance.

They all believed young Elias had died at the hands of SS in 1944.

He nearly did, several times.

"When I think back, it's a miracle I lived through it all," he says.

He remembers going with his mother to a German compound where he saw his father's battered body. Months later his mother died of malnutrition. "Our daily ration was a slice of bread and my mother starved herself so my sister Thimira and I would have food."

An older half-brother moved in. There was conflict between him and Lyn which led to the younger boy running away to fend for himself.

AHEAD lay many terrifying adventures. While he was foraging for food in a yard at Piraeus, near Athens, a gun battle between partisans and German troops broke out around him.

Hiding behind bins, he saw two partisans jump over a wall into the yard. They had been tipped off that a German officer was carrying a list of key members of the resistance.

They had killed the officer and

were now escaping with his briefcase containing the incriminating papers.

"The men saw me and asked me to hide the papers in my shirt and deliver them to a barber's shop.

"The Germans threw a grenade which killed one of the partisans and injured the other. The wounded man gave me a machine gun and told me to fire through the gate. I heard a scream and afterwards I heard I had killed one of the Germans.

The Germans killed the second partisan with another grenade, then they found Lyn and took him away for interrogation.

"They had found the empty briefcase and wanted to know if I had seen what happened to the papers.

"All this time I had the papers hidden in my shirt. They put me in a cell without a bed or lights for two or three days. I remember collapsing through weakness. I will never forget the big rats there.

"Afterwards I found that the interpreter was a member of the same resistance group as the two in the yard. He knew I hadn't told them anything.

"The next night the resistance attacked the camp in force. There were shouts outside my cell telling me to keep away from the door.

"Shots were fired at the lock, then men got me out, up steps, through a hole in the ceiling.

"I was pushed into a lorry, which drove out of the camp with the partisans throwing grenades as they went.

"The resistance man looking after me was killed and I got hit in the thigh, but we got away to the mountains where I was given a piggy-back to a cave which was their base."

There were huge celebrations when he handed over the papers.

A couple of months later, the partisans tried to rescue 22 hostages the Germans were about to execute in reprisal for resistance attacks.

"The resistance knew when the 22 hostages were to be machine-gunned. Their plan was that I would get into the compound disguised as a water-seller with two grenades inside my coat. As a child I wouldn't be suspected.

"I got into the yard and threw the grenades at the machine-gun. That was the signal for the resistance to attack, but a German threw a grenade at the hostages and some were killed.

"He then came towards me and I shot him with my pistol. We all scrambled aboard lorries and got away with the remaining hostages.

The resistance gave me a harmonica as a reward. I remember feeling very important."

Lyn stayed with the resistance at a cave where a young woman,

Evthoxia, became his "mother." One day the Germans attacked the cave. "We had been betrayed. Evthoxia was killed. I remember trying to wake her up. I loved her so much, in anger I took grenades from one of the dead men and hurled them towards the Germans.

"I hid among rocks. It was three days before I dared come down. From then on I was on my own, living on scraps among the ruins."

THE partisans killed two Germans close to where Lyn was hiding. "I found the bodies and took their boots, which I knew I could exchange for food. They were worth more than money. I hid them in the rocks while I went back for their guns.

"But SS soldiers suddenly appeared and caught me. I spat at one of them and he hit me across my face with his gun butt. It was 30 years before my jaw was put right.

"The Germans held me for several weeks, constantly interrogating me. They put me in a car and drove me off. I didn't know where they were taking me. Suddenly, partisans attacked and the driver was killed.

"The car turned over and in the confusion I ran off and escaped."

Lyn returned to Piraeus but soon found himself in the middle of yet another gun battle.

"I was lying on the ground between two dead Germans. I took one of their grenades and threw it into a building where there were two other Germans. One was killed but the other one lived long enough to tell other soldiers what had happened. They grabbed me along with some partisans and took us to a camp, where I was interrogated for several days.

"I was marched out into a yard where three men were already tied to posts, they tied me to a pole away

from the men and blindfolded me. I heard the order given to fire but the bullets didn't touch me. They were trying to make me talk by pretending they were going to kill me."

Lyn was then taken to the village of Kokkinia just outside Athens. It was August 17 1944.

He got away, and continued to eke out a precarious existence among ruins in Athens, at one time living with another boy in a cave-like hole in the walls of the Acropolis.

LATE in 1944, British troops occupied Athens, but not sooner had the Germans left when a ferocious civil war broke out. On December 3 there was a major clash between rival factions in the Greek capital.

"Shots were fired and a lot of people were killed. I remember running with a crowd with people dropping dead or injured around me.

"British troops were letting people into a hotel that they had occupied and I ran in. I was dizzy with malnu-

trition. I just crawled under the reception desk and passed out. Hours later I was woken up by Welch Regiment soldiers, who took care of me and nursed me back to health."

HE became the soldiers' mascot. They made him a cut-down sergeant's uniform and called him Titch.

A Captain Llewellyn Rowland, whose parents lived in Cathedral Road, Cardiff, took the boy under his wing and arranged his adoption by Leighton and Bess Rowland (no relation) who ran an opticians business in Bargoed. Lyn later went to Bargoed Grammar School.

He said, "Last year a friend persuaded me to go back and I spent a week there." It was a momentous week. A local TV station heard he was searching for wartime locations and filmed his quest. The film was screened after he returned to Cardiff.

"One evening I got a call from the producer, who said members of my family had contacted them after seeing the film. They all thought I had been killed by the Germans." Two weeks later Lyn was back in Greece. This time, as he stepped off the plane the family was there to greet him.

"It was tremendous. I was feted everywhere, staying with the Savoy and Dorchester hotels in London and the Queen's Hotel in St Mary Street, Cardiff.

He is seeking a publisher for the book he started writing in the 1970s but then put aside until recently.

In 1979 after a long search he found Capt Rowland, the soldier who helped arrange his adoption, retired and living in Cwmbran. Mr Rowland helped piece together some of the book, but died a few years later.

TRAUMA: Lyn Rowland – writing the book made him remember things he he would rather forget

SAVED: Lyn as 'Titch' the Welch Regiment mascot in 1944

Newspaper printed in 1995 about "Titch".

SOUTH WALES ECHO, WEDNESDAY, MARCH 21, 1

Together again 30 years after—Captain Llewellyn Rowland (left) and Titch. Below is the headline which brought them together again.

'Titch' keeps searching

Cardiff Officer "Adopts"

THE NIGHTMARE story of a young C
with only his wits to keep him ...

THE STROLLER

Titch finds his wartime hero again

AFTER YEARS of searching, Greek-born M
Lyn "Titch" Rowland, of Cardiff, has been re
united with the war-time officer who saved hi
life and brought him to South Wales.

The two men got together for the first time last week following an appeal in the South Wales Echo three weeks ago.

The officer was Capt. Llewellyn Rowland — no relation — of Cwmbran, who plays a vital role in a book being pieced together by Titch.

The autobiography revolves around the life of a young Greek boy who lived through horrifying experiences during the German occupation of Athens in World War II.

So far Titch has completed nearly two-thirds of the book at his Cathedral Road home, but his work came to a temporary standstill while he attempted to find Capt. Rowland.

The officer was serving with the Welch Regiment in Athens during the war, and not only saved Titch's life but made the 10-year-old youngster a mascot of the British military mess and later introduced him to South Wales and a new life. This was recorded at the time by the Echo.

Adopted

After the war they lost touch, as Titch was adopted by a Bargoed family and grew up working in the restaurant and catering trade.

A few months ago 47-year-old Titch decided to take some time off to write his book.

"I'm overjoyed at finding Capt. Rowland," he

said. "It was very difficu for me to complete part of the book which involve names and dates incidents in Athens
would also like to than the South Wales Echo fc making it all possible."

Capt. Rowland, wh lives in Smallbrook Clos Southville, Cwmbran, sa he would be acting as "sort of technical advise on the book."

"I have had a look at the manuscript, and it ha the makings of a very goo book and I'm only to pleased to help out. W were both very pleased t see each other after suc a long time," he added.

Pat digs for digs

PROFESSIONAL musici Pat Connelly has just be booked to play a summe season at the Coney Bea Ballroom, Porthcawl, and has contacted the Sou Wales Echo to tell us abo the thing which would ma his first season in Wales pe fect—a typical Welsh lac lady.

Pat plays the saxopho clarinet and flute, is anxic to scotch any image of t professional musician as "hippy" or riotous charact "You might say I am a re pectable gentleman," h said.

SOUTH WALES ECHO, WEDNESDAY, FEBRUARY 28, 1979

'Titch' keeps searching

Cardiff Officer "Adopts" Greek War Orphan

● TITCH, a ten-year-old Athens fed, warmed and comforted boy who lost in one blow Shirts and slacks were cut down

● Flashback ... from the South Wales Echo in 1945.

THE NIGHTMARE story of a young Greek boy with only his wits to keep him alive on the war-torn streets of Athens is being pieced together in Cardiff.

Today, nearly 40 years after the end of World War II, the 4½ years of terror experienced under the German occupation of Greece is being turned into a book by a person who lived through it.

Mr. Lyn Rowland, who adopted his name when he arrived in South Wales from Athens when the war finished, is writing the book at his Cathedral Road home in Cardiff.

The horrifying detail that has so far filled nearly two thirds of his book has come to a tem-

The Stroller

porary standstill while he attempts to trace a Cardiff-born officer who saved his life.

The man Mr. Rowland wants to find is Capt. Llewellyn Rowland, who is no relation, who was serving in Greece with the Welch Regiment. Captain Rowland, who would today be in his late 60's, was the second son o fthe late Sir John and Lady Rowland, of Cardiff.

A picture of Capt. Rowland and the young Mr. Rowland, nicknamed Titch, appeared in the South Wales Echo in 1945, a year after the youngster wandered ragged cold and hungry into the British military mess in Athens.

It was as a special protege of Captain Rowland that "Titch" was given a new lease of life and fresh horizons that were eventually to lead to South Wales.

Mr. Rowland, now 47, said he would "dearly love" to see the old captain again to help fill in the missing gaps in his book.

After living for a number of years with a family in Bargoed Mr. Roland has spent most of his working life in the restaurant and catering trade working throughout Britain. He is now taking time off to write his book.

Some of the excerpts from this book reveal just how horrifying Mr. Rowlands's childhood was.

He tell how his father ██████████ and ██ mother died of starvation; how he was buried alive for three days; wounded when attacked by a German patrol, and locked in a rat-infested cell.

The day a fire-eater turned up in town...

ALL the world's a stage ... but not many small countries get the chance to sample the best of international entertainment on their own doorsteps.

Wales is the exception, thanks to the vision of drama director Robin Howarth who is in Cardiff to finalise plans for the most ambitious theatre festival ever mounted here.

His Wales International Theatre Festival for Young People is about to attract more than 300 professional performers from 15 countries to bring their varied talents to the Principality.

The jugglers, fire-eaters, mime artists, dancers and actors will make their presence felt in places like Abergavenny Market and the streets of Aberystwyth as well as in Cardiff city centre.

Newspapers printed in 1979 about "Titch".

Family Tree - 1996

The names of my family from twenty six people for fifty years I never knew I had.
All from my sister and half brother's marriage.

Family number one
My niece Tina and husband Kostas.
Two grown up boys and one girl. Cristos - Dimitries and Maria.

Family number two
My niece Eleny not married no children.

Family number three
My nephew Panayiotis and wife Angelicky.
Three young boys Vangelis, Angelos and Thothoris.

Family number four
My nephew Bandelis and wife Angelicky.
Two boys and one girl
Vangelis, Monolis, and Demitra. (One more is on the way)

Family number five

My niece Thespina and husband Yianis.

Two boys and one girl.

Alexi - Panayiotis and Maria (One more on the way)

Family number six

My uncle - Vasilis and wife.

he is my mother's brother.

A total family of twenty six.

and two more on the way.

The reunion of his family. The five children from his sister and brother.

WELCOME HOME - 1995

The family of Demetra greet Elias at Athens airport in June 1995.